NEW YORK PRECINCTS

A curated guide to the city's
best shops, eateries, bars
and other hangouts

PIP CUMMINGS

Hardie Grant

TRAVEL

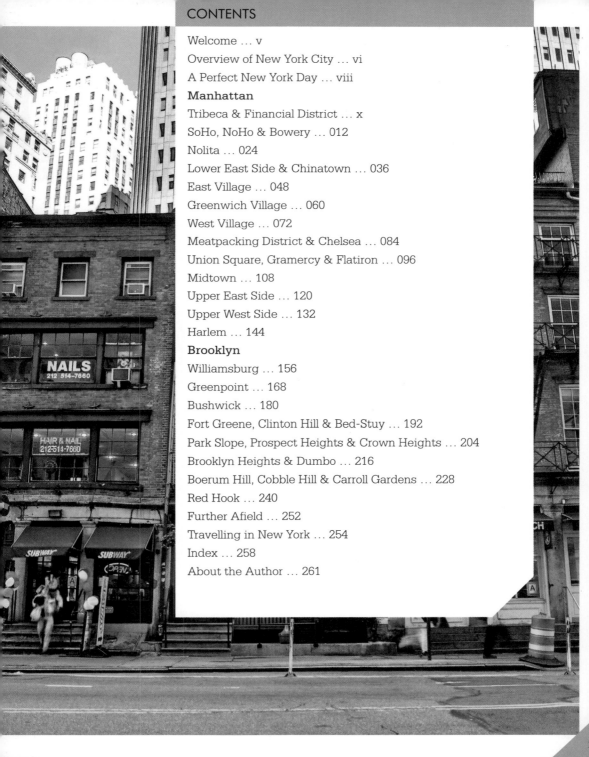

CONTENTS

WELCOME

Welcome to New York City – you've made it! You probably feel you know it already from hundreds of films and TV shows, but you'll soon discover it is full of surprises. This guide helps you make the most of the city's familiar cultural icons, as well as giving a local's tips to some more secret locales. It features my favourite places in each precinct – an insider guide to the best of New York's shops, cafes, restaurants and bars, as well as waterfronts and green spaces to catch your breath.

Manhattan's skyscrapers, yellow cabs, grand museums, orderly street grid and hectic street life are quintessential New York. More recently, visitors have been eager to head for Brooklyn, too – specifically Williamsburg. Brooklyn is actually a huge borough, and much of it is worth exploring. But Williamsburg and its neighbour, Greenpoint, exemplify the turn towards artisanal food and drinks from locally sourced ingredients, and the old-time fashion and decor that provide a beautiful counterbalance to Manhattan's fast pace and cosmopolitanism. Ideally, you'll find time to experience both.

New York is no longer the crime-ridden metropolis it once was, but its locals still carry an unwarranted reputation for toughness. Sure, they can be disarmingly direct but there's also a very old-fashioned courteousness here, including liberal uses of 'Sir' and 'Ma'am', and an optimism that is infectious. In America's most densely populated and most diverse city, you can expect to be constantly stimulated. Discover some of the world's greatest museums, sprawling urban parklands and architecture, or a new shop, bar or restaurant in which to dodge the slipstream for a little while.

After living here for seven years, I can honestly say there's not a day I'm not delighted by some unanticipated moment – a busker on the subway, a bold new piece of public art, the distinctive turn of the seasons, or an interaction between strangers. Keep your eyes up and your earphones out – your curiosity will definitely be rewarded and your heart and mind expanded.

Pip Cummings

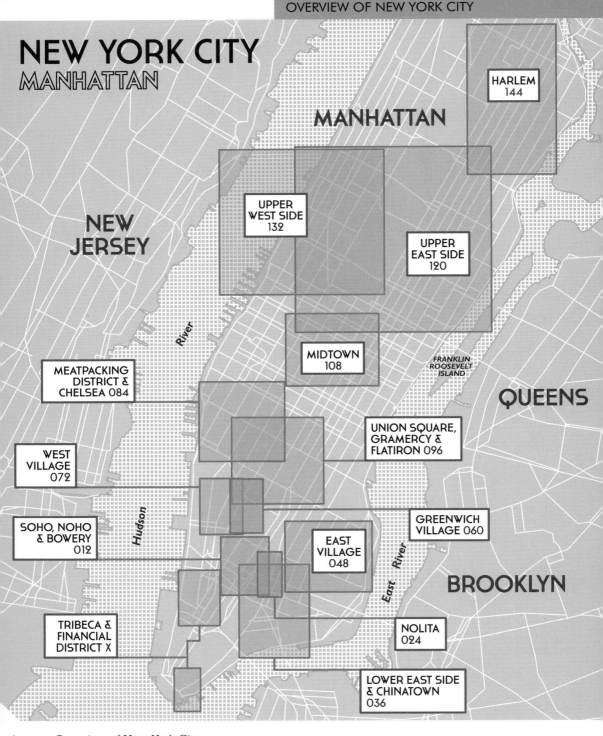

NEW YORK CITY
MANHATTAN

MANHATTAN

NEW JERSEY

QUEENS

BROOKLYN

HARLEM
144

UPPER
WEST SIDE
132

UPPER
EAST SIDE
120

MIDTOWN
108

FRANKLIN
ROOSEVELT
ISLAND

MEATPACKING
DISTRICT &
CHELSEA 084

River

UNION SQUARE,
GRAMERCY &
FLATIRON 096

WEST
VILLAGE
072

Hudson

GREENWICH
VILLAGE 060

SOHO, NOHO
& BOWERY
012

EAST
VILLAGE
048

East River

TRIBECA &
FINANCIAL
DISTRICT X

NOLITA
024

LOWER EAST SIDE
& CHINATOWN
036

MANHATTAN

QUEENS

GREENPOINT 168

BUSHWICK
180

WILLIAMSBURG 156

BROOKLYN
HEIGHTS
& DUMBO
216

BROOKLYN

RED
HOOK
240

BOERUM HILL,
COBBLE HILL
& CARROLL
GARDENS 228

PARK SLOPE,
PROSPECT HEIGHTS
& CROWN HEIGHTS
204

FORT GREENE,
CLINTON HILL
& BED-STUY 192

Hudson River

East River

BROOKLYN
NEW YORK CITY

A PERFECT NEW YORK DAY

New York is so vast and so packed with pleasures, you can have all sorts of 'perfect days' without covering a lot of miles. An ideal day for me could take in either Manhattan's high culture and buoyant energy, or the more diverse and creative neighbourhoods of Brooklyn.

A Manhattan day should start in SoHo with an indulgent breakfast at **Balthazar** (*see* p. 017), making sure to nab some snacks for later from their adjacent bakery. Then I'd wander the shopping mecca of **Broadway**, **Mercer** and **Greene Streets** and into tucked-away **Howard Street** (*see* p. 014) for some of the most innovative and inspiring shops, and a shot of caffeine at the retro-styled **Nickel and Diner**. From here, I'd catch the train to the **Museum Mile** and explore the **Metropolitan Museum of Art** (MoMA, *see* p. 118), then have lunch in the **Neue Museum**'s elegant **Café Sabarsky** (*see* p. 124). Afterwards, I'd cross the road into **Central Park** (*see* p. 130) to enjoy a ramble south-west towards **Columbus Circle** and catch the subway down to Chelsea and its edgy contemporary galleries, near the end of **The High Line** (*see* p. 094). In any season, there's no place in New York that still surprises me as much as this elevated park, full of semi-wild plantings, sculptures and viewing platforms. If I felt like a side stop of glamour, a champagne and a knock-out view of the Hudson River and city, I'd pop up to the **Top of The Standard** hotel (*see* p. 093). Having walked the Highline's length, I'd stroll the few blocks into the West Village among its lovely brownstones before claiming a table at the minuscule French restaurant **Buvette** (*see* p. 076) for an early dinner. Then a quick subway ride back up to the theatre district for a show, or an easy walk into Greenwich Village for music at the **Blue Note Jazz Club** (*see* p. 068) or stand-up at the **Comedy Cellar** (*see* p. 069). My favourite time to go up the **Empire State Building** to its 86th-floor viewing platform is around midnight, when the crowds have thinned out but there's still an hour until closing time. Then I'd circle back to the West Village for a nightcap at speakeasy **Employees Only** (*see* p. 080).

On weekends, I'm happy to enjoy a gentle day in Brooklyn. Brunch is a New York institution and I'd start the day with

a mezze feast with friends at Greenpoint's **Glasserie** (*see* p. 174) or in the garden at **Milk and Roses** (*see* p. 175). I'd follow with a slow browse through the shops of **Franklin Street** (*see* p. 170), before hopping on the East River ferry for the quick trip to **Smorgasburg** (*see* p. 166) in Williamsburg. With around 100 food vendors to buy from, this is a great place in the warm months to stop for lunch, views and people-watching in the park. In the colder months, I'd browse my favourite stores, including **Catbird** (*see* p. 158) and **Narnia Vintage** (*see* p. 158), and take in a movie with a meal (and a cheeky glass of wine) at the **Nitehawk Cinema** (*see* p. 166). Back on the ferry, I'd make my way down to Dumbo and walk via the waterfront to Brooklyn Heights, through the brilliant **Brooklyn Bridge Park** (*see* p. 226), allowing time for all of its remarkable reclaimed piers, with attractions from a roller rink to a vast wildflower garden. Ideally, I'd loop back to the pedestrian bridge up to the **Brooklyn Heights Promenade** (*see* p. 226) in time to catch a view of the sunset over Manhattan.

On a cold day, the fireplace at nearby **Friend of a Farmer** (*see* p. 224) is my favourite spot to pop in for a pre-dinner drink. Then I'd wander downhill for dinner at **Colonie** (*see* p. 220) and a nightcap at any one of the fun bars clustered around the intersection of **Henry Street** and **Atlantic Avenue** (*see* p. 225).

Brooklyn is so spread out, I could just as happily spend a day in the neighbourhoods near lush **Prospect Park** (*see* p. 214). An indulgent Mexican brunch from **Chavela's** (*see* p. 212) in Prospect Heights can be balanced out with a walk around the park or **Brooklyn Botanic Garden** (*see* p. 215), also checking what's on show at the **Brooklyn Museum** (*see* p. 214). Then a leisurely half-hour stroll via Vanderbilt Avenue's bars and ice cream shops (**Weather Up**, **Ample Hills Creamery**) to Clinton Hill would be rewarded with an early evening meal at Tuscan treasure **Locanda Vini e Olii** (*see* p. 198), followed by a movie or performance at the innovative **Brooklyn Academy of Music** (BAM, *see* p. 202).

Map Labels

TO MAP RIGHT
(VIA WHITEHALL
STREET & BROADWAY)

STONE STREET

BROAD STREET

PEARL STREET

BRIDGE STREET

WHITEHALL STREET

PEARL STREET

DEAD RABBIT
GROCERY
AND GROG

Vietnam
Veterans
Plaza

NYC
Parks

STREET

WATER

BROAD STREET

FINANCIAL
DISTRICT

WHITEHALL
STREET-
R W

STREET

SOUTH

SOUTH
FERRY

FDR DRIVE

Battery
Maritime
Building

Staten Island
Ferry
Whitehall
Terminal

TRIBECA &
FINANCIAL
DISTRICT

Tribeca ('Triangle below Canal Street')
is a former industrial area, colonised
by artists in the 1970s for its huge loft
spaces, and now boasting upscale
boutiques, hip bars and a vibrant dining
scene. It tops the list of most expensive
real estate in the city.

The neighbouring Financial District (FiDi) is home to
the New York Stock Exchange, the Federal Reserve
Bank and an affluent residential population. It has
America's tallest building (see p. 010) and the
breathtaking memorial site commemorating the
attacks of September 11, 2001 (see p. 010).

Chambers St; Franklin St

*Different station locations for different subway lines

24 JUN 5016

SHOP
1 PATRON OF THE NEW
2 THE MYSTERIOUS BOOKSHOP
EAT
3 LOCANDA VERDE
4 ARCADE BAKERY
5 BUBBY'S

17

EAT & DRINK
6 THE ODEON
DRINK
7 DEAD RABBIT GROCERY
AND GROG
8 SMITH AND MILLS

SMITH
AND
MILLS

LOCANDA
VERDE

BUBBY'S

GREENWICH STREET

BEACH STREET

STREET

ERICSSON PL

NORTH MOORE STREET

VARICK STREET

Saint John's Park

SAINT JOHN'S LANE

Tribeca Park

FRANKLIN STREET

TRIBECA

FRANKLIN

HUDSON STREET

LEONARD STREET

PATRON
OF THE
NEW

FRANKLIN STREET

HARRISON STREET

MANHATTAN

JAY STREET

STAPLE STREET

WORTH STREET

THOMAS STREET

BROADWAY

STREET

0   100 m

Washington Market Park

GREENWICH STREET

DUANE STREET

Duane Park

STREET

READE STREET

HUDSON

WEST

DUANE STREET

ARCADE
BAKERY

THE
ODEON

STREET

CHAMBERS STREET

WARREN STREET

Bogardus Garden

The Frederick Hotel

CHAMBERS
STREET
1 2 3

CHAMBERS

CHAMBERS
STREET
A C E

CHURCH STREET

READE STREET

STREET

MURRAY STREET

THE
MYSTERIOUS
BOOKSHOP

STREET

STREET

BROADWAY

TO
DEAD RABBIT
GROCERY
AND GROG
(SEE MAP LEFT)

City Hall Park

PATRON OF THE NEW
151 Franklin St
212 966 7144
www.patronofthenew.us
Open Tues–Sat 12–7pm,
Sun 12–6pm

If you love luxury fashion inspiration that's different from the norm, check out the curatorial brilliance of mother-and-son duo Lisa and Jonathan Pak, whose eye for the avant-garde has won them the loyalty of hip-hop royalty, elite athletes and entertainers. If your pocket isn't as deep, there's opportunity to buy affordable pieces in the form of accessories, caps, t-shirts, jewellery and beauty products – and significantly marked down sale items in the spirit of keeping the stock at peak freshness. Brands considered obscure outside fashion circles command the floor here, including Off-White, Enfants Riches Déprimés, Amiri, Fear of God, Faith Connexion, Midnight Studios, Local Authority and Craig Green.

LOCAL TIP
Huge discounts are the drawcard at seven-storey designer superstore **Century 21** (22 Cortlandt St, Financial District). Visit on weekday mornings to nab the bargains and beat the crowds.

THE MYSTERIOUS BOOKSHOP

58 Warren St
212 587 1011
www.mysteriousbookshop.com
Open Mon–Sat 11am–7pm

Solve a crime among the towering floor-to-ceiling shelving in the world's oldest and biggest bookstore focused on mystery, detective fiction, espionage, suspense and thrillers. It's also home to the biggest Sherlock Holmes collection in the world – made up of standard titles as well as pastiches and memorabilia, including records, posters and magazine articles. Other sub-genres featured include Scandi-crime, once-forgotten and newly reissued titles from small publishers, and a sizeable stock of bibliomysteries – in which the crime involves rare books, eccentric collectors, libraries, bookstores or manuscripts. Shop for signed first editions of new titles, collectable hardcovers, and titles issued by the in-house Mysterious Press.

3.

LOCANDA VERDE

377 Greenwich St
212 925 3797
www.locandaverdenyc.com
Open Mon–Thurs 7–11am,
11.30am–3pm & 5.30–11pm,
Fri 7–11am, 11.30am–3pm &
5.30–11.30pm, Sat 8am–3pm
& 5.30–11.30pm, Sun
8am–3pm & 5.30–11pm

Located inside Robert De Niro's Greenwich Hotel, this buzzy Italian restaurant has walls lined with paintings by the actor's late father, Robert Snr, establishing the soulful family values that also feature in chef Andrew Carmellini's rustic menu. The tavern-style eatery is open from morning till night, and welcomes a clientele as keen for the luxe sheep's milk ricotta with truffle honey and burnt orange toast at breakfast as for Carmellini's grandmother's ravioli at night, both moderately priced. For around two months at the end of the year, the dinner menu expands to include a three-course 'trufflepalooza' option, with truffles as a core ingredient of each dish – even featuring in a dessert. In the warmer months, watch the world go by from the patio, with a glass from the extensive list of Italian wines.

4.

ARCADE BAKERY

220 Church St
212 227 7895
www.arcadebakery.com
Open Mon–Fri 8am–4pm

It would be incredibly easy to pass by this office building without noticing an inconspicuous plaque signalling the presence of a discreet bakery inside, but don't make that mistake. Arcade Bakery, under French-trained Roger Gural, turns out some of the finest and freshest small-batch babka, pizza and viennoiserie in the city. It's hard to narrow down the choice between the custardy quiches, chocolate-walnut babka, a surprising vanilla baguette, and a simple pizza topped with buffalo mozzarella, crushed San Marzano tomatoes and Romano cheese. To nab one of Gural's sought-after signature laminated baguettes – a dense, chewy loaf, wrapped and baked inside a buttery croissant-like crust – you must arrive after noon, according to the strict oven schedule. There are really no bad choices here. Take your pick, order a coffee, and sit or stand at the small tables built into former display windows in the foyer.

3.

4.

4.

4.

3.

3.

5.

BUBBY'S

129 Hudson St
212 219 0666
www.bubbys.com
Open Sun–Thurs 8am–11pm,
Fri–Sat 8–12am

Named for the Yiddish term for a grandmother, this downtown diner is just as eager as your average Bubby to heap your plate with simple, comforting food. Launched in 1990 as a pie company, the Tribeca institution (which now has a second location in the Meatpacking District), serves meals all day, with a commitment to American food and a particular knack for breakfasts. You'll be sufficiently full well beyond lunchtime, whether you opt for a pile of chocolate-chip pancakes, huevos rancheros, or the duck and cranberry hash. The made-from-scratch fare also includes crispy chicken in flaky buttermilk biscuits, generous market salads, bacon mac 'n' cheese, and matzoh ball soup. The best bargain is the 'meat and three' dinner menu, which lets you choose one meat dish with two sides and a sauce, and – almost 30 years on – the home-baked pies remain reliably good.

6.

THE ODEON

145 West Broadway
212 233 0507
www.theodeonrestaurant.com
Open Mon–Tues 8am–11pm,
Wed–Fri 8–12am, Sat 10–12am,
Sun 10am–11pm

This classic New York eatery and its hearty menu remains reassuringly satisfying – from the Art Deco decor to the steak frites. Featured on the cover of Jay McInerney's novel, *Bright Lights, Big City*, the neon signage of the Odeon is a last vestige of the decadent 1980s, when the downtown brasserie scene first took off and the city's night owls graduated from disco dancing to table hopping. Slide onto a burgundy leather banquette or take a seat at the enormous bar, order one of the well-made cocktails, and consider the following universal favourites: frisée salad with lardon and bacon vinaigrette, French onion soup, a fluffy omelette, steak frites, and a classic crème brûlée for dessert. Brunch is reliably good here and, unlike many of the city's establishments, you can make a reservation.

5.

6.

5.

7.

DEAD RABBIT GROCERY AND GROG

30 Water St
646 422 7906
www.deadrabbitnyc.com
Open The Taproom Mon–Sun
11–4am, The Parlor Mon–Sat
5pm–2am, Sun 5pm–12am

What qualifies a bar to be named the best in the world? Dead Rabbit Grocery and Grog took out the coveted *Drinks International* (magazine) title in 2016 with the clever marriage of an Irish tavern with a sophisticated New York cocktail bar. It has the largest Irish whiskey collection in the U.S., a menu of more than 70 historically accurate cocktails, and 'food to diet for' – full Irish breakfast, lamb shepherd's pie, or crispy fish and chips with mushy peas. Belfast natives Sean Muldoon and Jack McGarry have created a fun space with the sawdust-strewn downstairs Taproom serving up craft beers and whiskeys, while upstairs the more seductive Parlor turns out superior cocktails, with an oyster happy hour on weeknights (5–7pm) and ragtime piano on Wednesdays. Purchase the graphic-novel style drinks menu, which tells the tale of John Morrissey – leader of the Irish-American Dead Rabbits street gang, which roamed the locale from the 1850s.

8.

SMITH AND MILLS

71 North Moore St
212 226 2515
www.smithandmills.com
Open Mon–Wed & Sun
11–2am, Thurs–Sat 11–3am

In the city that never sleeps, it's handy to know where you can get dinner and a drink until 2am. This unmarked hole-in-the-wall bar, built in an old carriage house, doesn't take reservations, but that's the only unfriendly thing about it – which is fitting, given co-owners Matt Abramcyk and Akiva Elstein (who also created **Employees Only**, *see* p. 080) have been friends since they were kids. The limited seating in the light industrial space all faces inward to encourage conversation, and the small-plate menu is designed to be shared. Pair a simple menu of classic cocktails (that includes a sensationally gingery Dark 'n' Stormy) with oysters on the half shell or the butcher's plate of charcuterie, and allow the tungsten lighting and Bauhaus-inspired interior to transport you to the 1930s. Odd as it sounds, don't miss a trip to the washroom for the decor alone; it was created from a 1902 bird-cage elevator and features a fold-down sink from an old train carriage.

7.

LOCAL TIP
From the Dead Rabbit team comes retro-Cuban themed **BlackTail** (22 Battery Pl), serving classic cocktails with a strong rum presence and channelling the spirit of Ernest Hemingway.

8.

385

Take in the panoramic city and harbour views from the three-storey **One World Observatory** atop the tallest building in the Western Hemisphere, **One World Trade Center** (285 Fulton St, www.oneworldobservatory.com). Ascend via the Sky Pod while watching a virtual skyline transform across the city's centuries of history. Adjacent is **The Oculus** – an architectural gem by Santiago Calatrava, housing a train station, plaza and shopping mall.

The National September 11 Memorial and Museum (also known as the **9/11 Memorial and Museum**, 180 Greenwich St) commemorates the almost 3000 people that were killed in the 2001 attacks, as well as the 1993 World Trade Center bombing. It's at the former location of the iconic Twin Towers, destroyed in 2001.

The striking **Aire Ancient Baths** (88 Franklin St) are modelled after a Graeco-Roman bathhouse, with soaring ceilings and four pools ranging from hot to ice cold, in a vast candlelit subterranean cavern. Book ahead as only 25 people are admitted at a time.

Grab supplies from the massive French food emporium **Le District** (225 Liberty St), then stretch your legs at **Pier 25** (West St and North Moore St), the longest pier in **Hudson River Park**, including an 18-hole miniature golf course, beach volleyball courts, a berthing area for historic ships, a skate park and a lawn.

Thirty giant, colour-changing illuminated fish move as if they were underwater at the unconventional **SeaGlass Carousel at The Battery** (State St and Water St).

Take in the water and sunset views at the massive **Pier A Harbor House** (22 Battery Place), where Battery Park meets the Hudson River. The ground floor of the stately 19th-century venue features a giant saloon, serving oysters, pub food and craft beers, and is surrounded by a promenade for outdoor dining. Upstairs is a suite of more intimate, themed bars.

Admission is free to the **National Museum of the American Indian** (1 Bowling Green), featuring a rich permanent collection as well as temporary exhibits of contemporary and historical art and artefacts. This Smithsonian Institute branch museum is housed in a beautiful Beaux Arts building.

The free **Staten Island Ferry** departs from Whitehall Terminal and is a wonderful way to see the Statue of Liberty from the water. The trip takes 25 minutes each way.

Tribeca is also home to some nifty architecture, both old and new, including the fire station from *Ghostbusters*, **Hook and Ladder 8** (14 North Moore St), and the **Unhistoric Townhouse** (187 Franklin St), by Australian architect Jeremy Edmiston, which features a wildly undulating brick facade.

The shopping mecca of SoHo ('south of Houston Street') sees grand cast-iron buildings home to a profusion of luxury boutiques (Greene and Mercer streets), chain stores (Broadway) and independent design showrooms. The legacy of this once industrial area's artist-led revival of the 1970s and '80s is found in its galleries, performance venues and film culture.

North of Houston (NoHo) is quieter, with intimate restaurants and bars, while bordering Bowery has become an edgy hub of art museums, performance venues and boutique hotels.

Canal St; Broadway–Lafayette St; Bleecker St; Spring St

*Different station locations for different subway lines

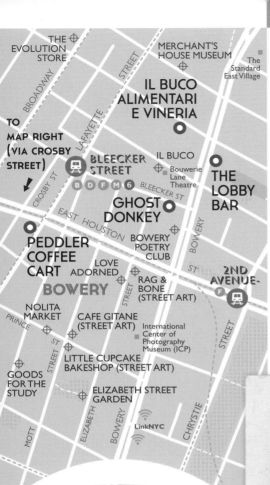

Map labels:
- THE EVOLUTION STORE
- MERCHANT'S HOUSE MUSEUM
- The Standard East Village
- IL BUCO ALIMENTARI E VINERIA
- TO MAP RIGHT (VIA CROSBY STREET)
- BLEECKER STREET
- IL BUCO
- Bouwerie Lane Theatre
- THE LOBBY BAR
- GHOST DONKEY
- EAST HOUSTON
- BOWERY POETRY CLUB
- PEDDLER COFFEE CART
- LOVE ADORNED
- RAG & BONE (STREET ART)
- BOWERY
- 2ND AVENUE
- NOLITA MARKET
- CAFE GITANE (STREET ART)
- International Center of Photography Museum (ICP)
- LITTLE CUPCAKE BAKESHOP (STREET ART)
- GOODS FOR THE STUDY
- ELIZABETH STREET GARDEN
- LinkNYC

ʃOHO, NOHO & BOWERY

24   JUN 8016

ʃHOP
1 HOWARD ʃTREET
2 CUSTOMISED CLOTHING

EAT
3 IL BUCO ALIMENTARI E VINERIA
4 BALTHAZAR
5 DOMINIQUE ANSEL BAKERY

DRINK
6 PEDDLER COFFEE CART
7 GHOST DONKEY
8 LOBBY BAR AT THE BOWERY HOTEL

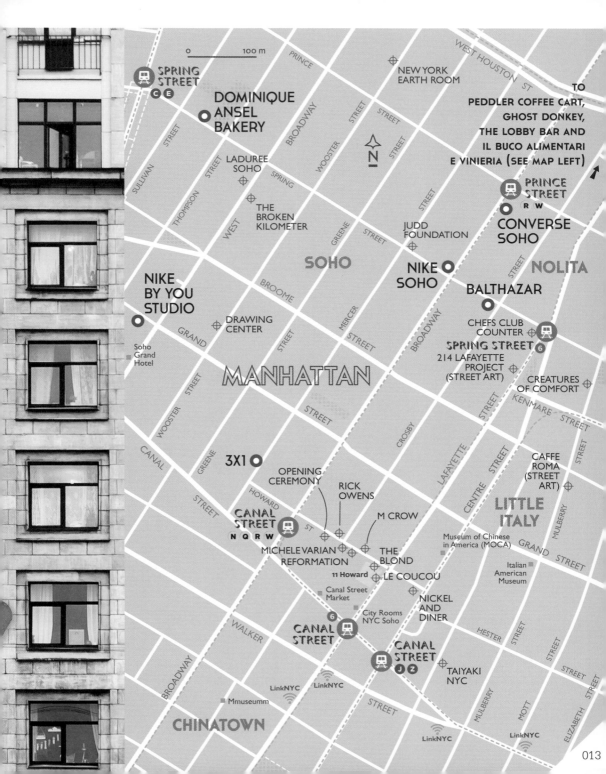

SPRING STREET
C E

DOMINIQUE ANSEL BAKERY

NEW YORK EARTH ROOM

TO PEDDLER COFFEE CART, GHOST DONKEY, THE LOBBY BAR AND IL BUCO ALIMENTARI E VINIERIA (SEE MAP LEFT)

LADURÉE SOHO

PRINCE STREET
R W

CONVERSE SOHO

THE BROKEN KILOMETER

JUDD FOUNDATION

SOHO

NIKE SOHO

NOLITA

BALTHAZAR

NIKE BY YOU STUDIO

DRAWING CENTER

CHEFS CLUB COUNTER

Soho Grand Hotel

SPRING STREET
6
214 LAFAYETTE PROJECT (STREET ART)

CREATURES OF COMFORT

MANHATTAN

CAFFE ROMA (STREET ART)

LITTLE ITALY

3X1

OPENING CEREMONY

RICK OWENS

M CROW

Museum of Chinese in America (MOCA)

CANAL STREET
N Q R W

MICHELE VARIAN REFORMATION

THE BLOND

11 Howard

LE COUCOU

Italian American Museum

Canal Street Market

NICKEL AND DINER

City Rooms NYC Soho

CANAL STREET
6

CANAL STREET
J Z

TAIYAKI NYC

LinkNYC   LinkNYC

Mmuseumm

CHINATOWN

LinkNYC   LinkNYC

0   100 m

N

013

HOWARD STREET, SOHO

Howard Street is a discreet pleasure, with its concentration of imaginative shops and eateries.

Opening Ceremony (no. 35) takes its inspiration from the modern Olympics, merging merchandise from a 'visiting country' with the edgier work of iconic and emerging home-grown designers. Across four storeys you'll find shoes, a children's corner, a bookshop and multiple floors of women's clothing. Sale items are regularly slashed to around half price. A second shop next door (no. 33) focuses on menswear.

Former fashion designer **Michele Varian** (no. 27) is known for her handmade decorative pillows, but her edgy home and lifestyle store also offers jewellery, candles and other curiosities, much of it with a gently Gothic aesthetic.

The flagship store of eco-chic brand **Reformation** (no. 23) sells sexy, feminine clothing (think deep necklines, short hems, flowy skirts) made from deadstock fabrics, as well as one-off vintage pieces revamped to bring them up to date. Cool-girl fans of the label include Taylor Swift, Karlie Kloss and Rihanna.

Michele Lamy – wife, muse and creative accomplice of **Rick Owens**, whose store bears his name, (no. 30) – designed this colossal space of concrete, mirror and steel. Find runway and ready-to-wear pieces to sub-label DRKSHDW, and Lamy's own Hunrod jewellery.

From handmade roasting sticks for marshmallows to a bear bolo tie, furniture designer Tyler Hays has the urban mountain-man aesthetic covered at **M Crow** (no. 16), which is named after a 107-year-old general store in his home town of Lostine, Oregon. The multi-roomed wonderland is stocked entirely with goods handmade in Hays' Philadelphia studio.

Boutique hotel **11 Howard** (no. 11) incorporates both the lavish lounge bar **The Blond** (with a velvet rope and doorman from 10pm) and immaculate French dining palace **Le Coucou**. Under chef Daniel Rose, Le Coucou took out America's coveted 'Best New Restaurant' gong from the James Beard Foundation in 2017. You can book up to a month in advance, but be open to dining very early or late – it's considered the most difficult and desirable reservation to secure in New York.

Fashioned after a 1950s luncheonette but serving ultra-contemporary comfort food, **Nickel and Diner** (no. 1) is the place for cold-brew coffee, zesty buttermilk pancakes or tempura-battered fried chicken with a side of nostalgia.

CUSTOMISED CLOTHING, SOHO

For the ultimate souvenir from New York, try a fully customised pair of jeans or trainers.

At **Converse SoHo** (560 Broadway), dream up a unique pair of Chuck Taylors, decorated with your own artwork or one of 150 ever-changing graphics, and swap out the eyelets, shoelaces and rubber toecap. Book an hour-long session with a designer, and your shoes will be produced the same day.

At **3x1** (15 Mercer St), a glass-walled factory reveals 24 machinists creating custom and bespoke jeans that range from hundreds of dollars to more than $1500. At the lower end, select from in-season designs and customise details like denim wash, thread, buttons and rivets. For top dollar you get bespoke – choose denims and tailor the fit, pockets and trims. Note that the garments take several weeks to create.

To visit the **Nike By You Studio** (45 Grand St) you download the Nike app and get an invitation to participate in the Nike Maker Experience – a one-on-one session personalising a pair of Presto Xs, made on-site in under an hour. Nike also offers NBA and NFL jersey customisation at the **Nike SoHo** store (529 Broadway), by appointment only.

3.

IL BUCO ALIMENTARI E VINERIA

53 Great Jones St
212 837 2622
www.ilbucovineria.com
Open Mon–Thurs 8am–11pm,
Fri 8–12am, Sat 9–12am, Sun
9am–11pm (dining room from
5.30pm till closing)

Communal dining here feels as if you chanced upon a trattoria proudly showcasing local produce while on tour through provincial Italy. Entry is via the alimentari part of this dining–delicatessen hybrid, which sells house-made bread, cured meats, imported olive oils and vinegars, and artisanal dry goods. Breakfast and lunch, including an outstanding slow-roasted short rib panino, are served here, and it converts from coffee bar to wine bar around noon. Down a few steps, you're delivered to a buzzy dining room, which declares the venue's total commitment to sustainability by repurposing joists from its former lumber warehouse into bar panelling and furnishings, cutting boards and salumi platters.

The house-made breads, salumi, pastas and gelati are not to be missed, and try the tender salt-baked whole branzino (European bass) and the short ribs for two, crusted with peppercorns and coriander seeds.

LOCAL TIP
If it's a date night, book well in advance for the intimate farmhouse ambience of the original **Il Buco** (47 Bond St), serving rustic Mediterranean–Italian fare in a former antique shop since 1994.

BALTHAZAR

80 Spring St
212 965 1414
balthazarny.com
Open Mon–Thurs 7.30–12am,
Fri 7.30–1am, Sat 8–1am,
Sun 8–12am

Here is a fantasy of Paris in New York. It's as glorious and bustling now as it was when it took the local dining scene by storm in 1997. Serving traditional French bistro food from breakfast until supper daily (brunch on weekends), it specialises in fresh seafood and shellfish – including the grandiose three-tiered 'Le Balthazar' platter.

What you forfeit in space – the 180 seats are crammed into the faux fin-de-siècle space – you gain in people-watching. Meals are pricey, even breakfast, but you are gaining a total experience – from the bestselling steak frites to the golden lighting and attentive service. Booking is advised – and on the early side if you want to avoid the late-night sound levels. Breakfast may actually be Balthazar's finest hour.

Attached is a tiny bakery selling soups, salads and sandwiches, and their esteemed breads and pastries, including an orange-inflected brioche, delicately crusted canelés, and tartines of caramelised apple in puff pastry.

5.
DOMINIQUE ANSEL BAKERY
189 Spring St
212 219 2773
https://dominiqueansel.com
Open Mon–Sat 8am–7pm,
Sun 9am–7pm

It was while I was living in SoHo in 2013 that Dominique Ansel launched his trademarked 'Cronut', provoking a line of croissant-hybrid enthusiasts to form halfway around the block from early morning until the daily stock was depleted. A bouncer was deployed, scalpers emerged, and even celebrities couldn't jump the queue.

Years later, the line persists, sustained by the short supply (around 350 a day), the limit of two per customer and the never-to-be-repeated flavours, which change monthly. A 'Cronut 101' guide on the bakery website recommends arriving before 7.30am (earlier on weekends); or go online on Monday at 11am to try to pre-order up to six Cronuts, two weeks ahead.

Ansel has also brought fun to the Paris–New York – a twist on the Paris–Brest, made with chocolate, caramel and peanut butter filling in choux pastry – and is lauded for his kouign amann (caramelised croissants). For all these, plus savoury lunch fare, you can sail past the queue.

6.
PEDDLER COFFEE CART
Cnr Lafayette and Houston sts
646 645 2225
https://nypdlr.com
Open Mon–Fri 7.30am–5pm

Witty Australian entrepreneur Byron Kaplan has managed to revolutionise that most ubiquitous of New York icons, the coffee cart – not just by serving superior espresso, from cortados to flat whites, but by creating a temporary outlet that is more like a bricks-and-mortar experience. Against the city's unyielding 'time is money' ethos, Peddler's coffee is made from freshly ground, high-quality beans and served in mismatched cups or glass tumblers to customers persuaded to stop a while on one of the business's colourful plastic stools.

Evidence of Kaplan's playful vision can also be found in Peddler's range of merchandise, which includes a rainbow-striped propeller hat, embroidered mischievously with Donald Trump's presidential campaign slogan, 'Make America Great Again'.

LOCAL TIP
If French patisseries are your weakness, visit **Ladurée SoHo** (398 West Broadway), a full-service restaurant with a special teatime menu, including its famous macarons, shipped weekly from Paris.

7.
GHOST DONKEY

4 Bleecker St
212 254 0350
www.ghostdonkey.com
Open Mon–Sun 5pm–2am

This fairylight-festooned tequila and mezcal bar is a joyfully decadent experience, from the shots served with curated salts to the inspired bar snacks.

In addition to the imaginative cocktail menu – featuring a funky huitlacoche mushroom-infused mezcal margarita, and playful salted caramel horchata – the homage to all things Mexican extends to their nachos menu, including mole chicken and black truffle varieties. Cinnamon churros will satisfy sweet-toothed patrons.

The bar's namesake drink, El Burro Fantasma, is a fruity, chilli-rich indulgence made for two and served in a festive ceramic donkey. The bar has limited seating, so arrive early if you plan to eat. With a reputation for being a great place to kick off an even bigger night, the space soon fills up in the evenings.

8.
LOBBY BAR AT THE BOWERY HOTEL

335 Bowery
212 505 9100
www.theboweryhotel.com
Open Sun–Wed 5pm–2am,
Thurs–Sat 5pm–4am

There's a slightly eccentric gentlemen's club feel to the decor at this opulent space, where entry can be hit-and-miss because priority goes to hotel patrons and their guests. If you get in, the experience is always rewarding – the celebrity-spotting (mostly film and rock'n'roll talent) is fun, the service is great and the drinks are reassuringly old-fashioned.

The luxurious wood-panelled room features Persian rugs, velvet armchairs, church pews, taxidermied deer heads, paintings of hounds, vases of peacock feathers and a painted frieze of old New York – all transporting you to a different era. In the cold months, forego the very respectable cocktail list and instead order a hot mulled wine to enjoy by the stone fireplace.

Even when you can't get in, it's always possible to drink at the smaller bar, adjacent to the large parlour room, which has a long, zinc-topped bar and a knowledgeable bartender.

WHILE YOU'RE HERE

Film Forum (209 West Houston St, SoHo) screens foreign art and American independent films, and a program of classics, documentaries and directors' retrospectives.

Book in advance for the small guided tours of artist Donald Judd's five-storey home (**Judd Foundation**, 101 Spring St, SoHo), featuring his custom-made furniture and art collection, with works by Marcel Duchamp and Frank Stella, and a 1969 Dan Flavin neon sculpture running the length of Judd's bedroom.

Ring the doorbell at 141 Wooster St, SoHo and proceed to the second floor to see a strangely calming artwork, created by Walter de Maria in 1977. The **New York Earth Room** is a 60cm layer of soil that covers the greater part of a multimillion-dollar loft. Another secret sanctuary,

created by de Maria in 1979, is **The Broken Kilometer** (393 West Broadway, SoHo). This surprising work – 500 shiny brass rods, lined up in the appearance of perfect intervals – fills an entire cavernous room, a block deep.

The power of the pen (and pencil) is celebrated at the multistorey **Drawing Center** (35 Wooster St, SoHo), which presents works by contemporary and emerging artists as well as a program of artists' talks and film screenings.

Cruise more than 40 indoor stalls for art, fashion, vintage wares and souvenirs at the **Artists & Fleas** market (568 Broadway, SoHo), or check out the street vendors who sell jewellery, posters and other handmade pieces along West Broadway, Broadway or Spring Street (between Broadway and West Broadway).

The **Merchant's House Museum** (29 East 4th St, NoHo) offers ghost tours (and other tours) of the 1832 home, said to be 'Manhattan's most haunted house'. The collection of more than 3000 items, from furnishings to clothing, belonged to the Tredwells, a wealthy merchant-class family who lived here from 1835 to 1933.

The Hole (312 Bowery, The Bowery) is a huge independent art space where innovative art is accompanied by a dilettantish social scene. On the way you'll pass *Bowery Mural* (76 East Houston St, NoHo) – a huge wall that in the late 1970s bore a Keith Haring work, and that changes regularly.

Hear poetry performed – from slams to works in the poet's native language – at **Bowery Poetry Club** (308 Bowery, The Bowery) every Sunday and Monday.

The Public Theater (425 Lafayette St, NoHo) shows new and provocative plays, and is where *Hamilton* first played before moving to Broadway and becoming the hottest ticket in town. Heavily discounted rush tickets are often available an hour before the performance. **Joe's Pub**, a performance space within the Public Theater, hosts music, dance and comedy shows in a cabaret-style room with a terrific menu and table service.

Neighbourhood treasure **The Evolution Store** (687 Broadway, NoHo) is like a miniature museum of natural history, but one where everything is for sale – from scorpion lollipops to 4-billion-year-old meteorites and German botanical posters. Avoid if taxidermy offends.

TO MAP RIGHT (VIA ELIZABETH STREET)

KENMARE

STREET

LinkNYC

BOWERY

BOWERY

BROOME

STREET

LinkNYC

STREET

RANDOLPH BEER

ELIZABETH

STREET

BOWERY

GRAND STREET

Best Western Bowery Hanbee Hotel

LinkNYC

NOLITA

Once the domain of Italian butchers, bakeries and churches, Nolita (North of Little Italy) retains its old-world character in small walk-up buildings – now home to cosy cafes and independent designers. Nolita's quaint streets are adorned with colourful murals and the rich selection of street art (see p. 034) is always changing

On weekends, the Nolita Market (see p. 034) stree vendors line Prince Street selling jewellery and art, and pavement seating offers a great opportunity fo people-watching in the fashionable neighbourhood

Broadway–Lafayette St; Bleecker St; Spring St; Bowery

*Different station locations for different subway lines

24   JUN 8076

SHOP
1 LE LABO
2 MCNALLY JACKSON
3 VINT & YORK

EAT
4 CAFE GITANE
5 CHEFS CLUB

EAT & DRINK
6 THE WINE ROOM AT PLEASANT
7 RANDOLPH BEER

17

BROADWAY-
LAFAYETTE
STREET
🚇 B D F M 6

0 ———— 50 m

N

EAST HOUSTON STREET

CROSBY STREET

STREET

LAFAYETTE

JERSEY STREET

CHEFS
CLUB

MOTT STREET

ELIZABETH STREET

BOWERY STREET

BOWERY
MURAL

LOVE
ADORNED

RAG & BONE
(STREET ART)

MANHATTAN

MCNALLY
JACKSON

NOLITA
MARKET

VINT &
YORK

PRINCE STREET

CAFE
GITANE

International
Center of
Photography
Museum
(ICP)

JOHN
FLUEVOG
SHOES
(STREET
ART)

LE LABO

BOWERY

LITTLE
CUPCAKE
BAKESHOP
(STREET ART)

MULBERRY STREET

STREET

STREET

GOODS
FOR THE
STUDY

NOLITA

STREET

NEW
MUSEUM

ELIZABETH
STREET
GARDEN

SPRING STREET

MOTT STREET

DeSalvio
Playground

THE WINE
ROOM AT
PLEASANT

LinkNYC
📶

CREATURES OF
COMFORT

STREET

BOWERY

LinkNYC
📶

TO
RANDOLPH BEER
(SEE MAP LEFT)
↓

025

1.

LE LABO

233 Elizabeth St
212 219 2230
www.lelabofragrances.com
Open Mon–Sun 11am–7pm

- -

As the name suggests, this store is a tiny laboratory, turning out a range of freshly hand-blended perfumes on demand.

Styled like an old-time apothecary, with pressed metal walls, wooden specimen cabinets and attentive mixologists, the store's inventory also includes body lotions, massage oils and vegan candles.

Each scent is named for its most prominent note and the number of ingredients in the composition, from Ambrette 9 to Vetiver 46. There's also a second collection of 11 scents, only available over the counter as 'city exclusives'.

New York City's designated scent is Tubereuse 40, a citrusy-floral blend with dominant notes of neroli and tuberose – snap one up as a gift or souvenir. You can have the label personalised and printed on the spot.

LOCAL TIP
Don't miss the intriguing
clothing, jewellery and
lifestyle products at
Creatures of Comfort
(205 Mulberry St)
and **Love Adorned**
(269 Elizabeth St).

2.

MCNALLY JACKSON

52 Prince St
212 274 1160
www.mcnallyjackson.com
Open Mon–Sat 10am–10pm,
Sun 10am–9pm

The inventory of 55,000 books at this two-storey independent bookshop includes a strong selection of children's, travel and coffee-table books, plus a large (and achingly seductive) cookbook selection.

Genre specialist staff will help you navigate the sometimes quirky categorisation, like literature shelved by country.

You can also use the Espresso Book Machine to print out a paperback in minutes, selecting from a list of millions of public domain titles.

Owner Sarah McNally – whose parents ran Canada's largest chain of independent bookshops – capitalises on her pedigree and the store's central location to cultivate a brilliant calendar of readings, signings and discussions. Expect to see, at no cost, literary luminaries reading to a packed room.

The store also sells periodicals on art, fashion, writing and design, which you can enjoy immediately at the defiantly wi-fi–free on-site cafe.

LOCAL TIP
Stationery fetishists should visit McNally's complementary 'life of the mind' store, **Goods for the Study** (234 Mulberry St), which sells new and vintage office supplies.

touch the
displa...

VINT & YORK
247 Elizabeth St
800 846 9915
www.vintandyork.com
Open Mon–Sat 11am–7pm,
Sun 12–6pm

A pair of glasses can be as transforming as a hat, a bold new lipstick or a pair of statement earrings, and vintage specs are a hot trend that shows no signs of diminishing. Unfortunately, the real thing can be hard to source or may have fallen victim to the ravages of age. This 'new vintage' design house is an e-commerce brand offering a flagship bricks-and-mortar store. It takes inspiration from the 1920s, then manufactures frames in high-quality celluloid acetate and nickel-free metal to sell at competitive prices ($109 to $149).

Channel Audrey Hepburn in the Cat's Meow frames, or James Dean – with a faux bois (imitation wood) twist – in the Way Out, or try the rather dandy Fitzgerald or flapper-esque Zelda styles.

The store offers on-site eye exams and a one-hour turnaround while you wander Nolita's quaint streets. No problem if you can't spare the time – all frames can be shipped worldwide.

4.
CAFE GITANE

242 Mott St
212 334 9552
www.cafegitanenyc.com
Open Mon–Sun 8.30–12am

When you're the grande dame of the local hipster hangouts, you get to call the shots and Cafe Gitane has some strict policies: no reservations, no mobile phones, and no laptops at lunchtime or after 7pm.

Two decades after it opened, the simple French–Moroccan menu is still reliably filling and reasonably priced. Staples include spicy merguez sausages paired with a tower of vegetable couscous, and hachis parmentier – a French version of shepherd's pie, made with fluffy mashed potatoes baked on top of ground beef and a creamy sauce.

The unfussy food goes well with the cosy retro decor, from chequered floors and Formica tables, to the yellow vintage cash register, French signage and knick-knacks. It's hard to go past the baked eggs for breakfast, paired with an espresso or even a glass of champagne, as you enjoy the passing show of artists and fashionistas.

5.
CHEFS CLUB

275 Mulberry St
212 941 1100
www.chefsclub.com
Open Mon–Sat 5.30–10.30pm

There's a theatre to this restaurant, where the open kitchen plays to an avid audience every night and each menu has a limited run. The concept turns the recent trend for food pilgrimages on its head by inviting celebrated chefs from around the world to take turns designing the menu, for between three weeks and three months, or to contribute a signature dish to an 'all-star' menu. Their recipes are then executed by a team, led by 20-year Alain Ducasse veteran Didier Elena. Expect greatest hits from the likes of Gabriel Rucker (Le Pigeon), Ori Menashe (Bestia) and J.J. Johnson (The Cecil).

The stylish space is housed in the landmark Puck Building, with brick walls, a vaulted ceiling atop immense columns, and tables arranged so diners can see the food being prepared. There is also a more intimate kitchen studio, where 24 guests can experience the creativity of renowned and emerging chefs up close.

Sign up to its newsletter to get ahead of the curve on who's up next.

LOCAL TIP

At the more casual **Chefs Club Counter** (62 Spring St), customers can order 'fine-fast' food at a counter and get a buzzer alert when it's ready.

5.

5.

4.

6.

THE WINE ROOM
AT PEASANT

194 Elizabeth St
212 965 9511
www.peasantnyc.com/about/
the-winebar
Open Tues–Sat 7pm–late

It's easy enough to overlook the steep and narrow staircase that leads to this un-signposted enoteca below Frank DeCarlo's beautifully rustic osteria, Peasant.

The subterranean wine room was designed with romance, friendship and, above all, conversation in mind, with large tables, candlelight, feel-good music and a great selection of Italian wines.

Because the entire menu of the upstairs restaurant is also available down here, stopping in for a drink with a friend often evolves into a relaxed, impromptu dinner. Pair a generous glass of Barolo with fresh burrata and tomatoes, split a deceptively simple margherita pizza, and before you know it you've found room for house-made lasagne with braised rabbit ragu. *Salute.*

RANDOLPH BEER
343 Broome St
www.randolphbeer.com
Open Sun–Tues 11–12am,
Wed–Fri 11–2am

Randolph Beer is a vast temple to American artisanal beer. Here, brew lovers can choose between 36 craft draughts pulled from 48 tap lines, which are customised to deliver each style of beer at its optimal temperature, and a reserve list of 37 limited or uncommon bottled beers. The shorter wine list is more continental.

Generosity is the signature style here – not just in the range of beers and the size of the room, but in the large booths, the Americana–road trip decor, the long bar and the portion sizes of the 'evolved comfort food'.

Take your time over Southern fried catfish sliders, a big-ass pretzel, maple bacon sprouts or, for vegetarians, the lauded garden burger. Each menu item comes with a beer-style recommendation, and many dishes are designed to share.

A 'bottomless brunch' special is available on weekends – one main and as much vodka-based punch or beer, or as many bloody marys or mimosas, as you care to drink in a 90-minute sitting.

One notable quirk of this otherwise easy-going establishment: they don't accept payment in cash.

In a quiet block of Elizabeth Street, between Prince and Spring streets, you'll find **Elizabeth Street Garden** – an enchanting green space a block deep, decorated with architectural remnants and statuary from the adjacent Elizabeth Street Gallery. Open during the middle of the day, it's a gentle place that's perfect for enjoying some downtime with a take-away coffee or lunch.

From Friday to Sunday between March and December, the footpath along Prince Street (between Mulberry and Mott streets) fills with artisans selling unique jewellery, screen-printed t-shirts, paintings, greeting cards and more at the **Nolita Market**.

New York is well-known for it's amazing street art, and there are several established street art locations to check out in the neighbourhood, all hosting permanent or rotating murals: **214 Lafayette Project** (214 Lafayette St), **Rag & Bone** (73 East Houston St), **Cafe Gitane** (242 Mott St), **Little Cupcake Bakeshop** (236 Mott St), **Caffe Roma** (176 Mulberry St) and **John Fluevog Shoes** (250 Mulberry St).

For 11 days every September, Mulberry Street between Canal

and Houston streets is transformed for a celebration of the **Feast of San Gennaro**, patron saint of Naples. Live music, delicious food, colourful parades and cannoli- and meatball-eating competitions dominate the festivities.

The seven-storey **New Museum** (235 Bowery, Nolita) houses three main gallery floors and a theatre, focused on emerging and under-recognised contemporary artists. Past shows have included a three-storey slide installed by Carsten Holler, and large-scale immersive video works by Pipilotti Rist. The museum is open every day but Monday. Visit the website (www.newmuseum.org) to find out about the latest exhibitions.

Indie band fans should check the line-up at rock bar and city staple **Bowery Ballroom** (6 Delancey St, Nolita) – the city's best venue for seeing indie acts, with great acoustics and a spacious downstairs lounge bar.

The Lower East Side's restless energy remains undiminished even though its gritty immigrant and punk history is all but erased now by fashionable bars and restaurants, small galleries and curated boutiques. The area has been settled by artists, designers and culinary pioneers, drawn to the creative community and bustling foot traffic.

Despite creeping gentrification, Chinatown remains a vibrant hub, full of dumpling houses and noodle joints, bakeries and karaoke bars, backstreet temples and elderly outdoor tai chi practitioners, where Mandarin is the default language in most stores.

 Delancey St; Grand St; Canal St

*Different station locations for different subway lines

Map labels

CANAL STREET
HESTER STREET
WALKER STREET
CANAL STREET
TAIYAKI NYC
TONY MOLY
LinkNYC
CANAL STREET
TO MAP RIGHT (VIA CANAL STREET)
CENTRE STREET
MULBERRY STREET
MOTT STREET
ELIZABETH STREET
BAYARD STREET
BAXTER STREET
Columbus Park
STREET
PELL STREET
BOWERY
WORTH STREET
NOM WAH TEA PARLOR
CHINESE TUXEDO
DIVISION STREET
CATHERINE STREET
PARK ROW
OLIVER STREET

LOWER EAST SIDE & CHINATOWN

SHOP
1 Tictail Market
2 Assembly New York
3 Tony Moly

EAT
4 The Fat Radish
5 Dimes
6 Chinese Tuxedo

DRINK
7 Casa Mezcal
8 Mr Fong's

CAFE GITANE (STREET ART)

International Center of Photography Museum (ICP)

Gatsby Hotel

Sunshine Cinema

KATZ'S DELICATESSEN

LITTLE CUPCAKE BAKESHOP (STREET ART)

Sara D. Roosevelt Park

STANTON STREET

NEW MUSEUM

BOWERY

ASSEMBLY NEW YORK

ELIZABETH STREET GARDEN

BOWERY

CHRISTIE STREET

FORSYTH

RIVINGTON

ELDRIDGE

ALLEN

STREET

LINKNYC

ECONOMY CANDY

KENMARE ST

BOWERY BALLROOM

ELIZABETH STREET

DELANCEY

RUSS & DAUGHTERS CAFE

ESSEX STREET MARKET

J Z BOWERY

LinkNYC

Best Western Bowery Hanbee

BROOME

LOWER EAST SIDE TENEMENT MUSEUM

DELANCEY STREET

F M

STREET

TICTAIL MARKET

J Z

GRAND STREET

B D

GRAND

STREET

ESSEX STREET

CASA MEZCAL

BOWERY

CHRISTIE

Sara D. Roosevelt Park

STREET

ALLEN

ORCHARD

LUDLOW STREET

ESSEX

NORFOLK ST

STREET

HESTER

STREET

GRAND STREET

Mahayana Buddhist Temple

ELDRIDGE

LinkNYC

THE FAT RADISH

METROGRAPH CINEMA

Seward Park

LOWER EAST SIDE

MUSEUM AT ELDRIDGE STREET

Hotel Richland New York

N

TO TONY MOLY & CHINESE TUXEDO (SEE MAP LEFT)

DIMES

STREET

LinkNYC

EAST BROADWAY

DIMES DELI

CHINATOWN

EAST BROADWAY

MANHATTAN STREET

BROADWAY

PIKE

HENRY

RUTGERS

EAST BROADWAY

F

STREET

MANHATTAN

MR FONG'S

BRIDGE STREET

STREET

STREET

MADISON STREET

MADISON

0   100 m

1.

TICTAIL MARKET
90 Orchard St
917 388 1556
https://tictail.com/tictail-market
Open Mon–Sat 12–9pm,
Sun 12–6pm

Until recently, Tictail was an online-only marketplace, founded in Sweden. After experimenting with pop-up shops in Paris, Stockholm and New York, the brand found its spiritual and physical home among the creatives of the Lower East Side.

The ultra-Scandinavian interior is the backdrop for a curated range that is refreshed weekly, drawing from the more than two million art, fashion and home decor products available on the site. On a recent visit, I saw earrings by a German goldsmith, Swedish-designed streetwear made in Burkina Faso from African textiles, and a blouse from an LA fashion label run by first-generation Latinas. The shop's only permanent offering is By Mutti porcelain – classic pieces decorated with imagery from sailor tattoos, created by Tictail founder Carl Waldekranz's mother, Eva Gernandt.

One of the loveliest features of this consciously community-building retail experience is a 'bio wall' at the back of the store, featuring photos of various artisans, accompanied by creator statements.

2.

ASSEMBLY NEW YORK
170 Ludlow St
212 253 5393
www.assemblynewyork.com
Open Mon–Sat 11am–7pm,
Sun 12–6pm

- -

Assembly is more like a brash indie art gallery than a boutique. Everything is meticulously selected and displayed in the white-on-white interior. Browse to a Grace Jones soundtrack among the reconstructed denim, sunglasses and scents, with brilliant pops of vintage scattered among global brand garments.

This is the vision of former Angeleno Greg Armas, who has blended the store's own line (including its iconic inverted New York logo t-shirts) with an eclectic mix – shoes by Reike Nen, fragrance by Maison Louis Marie and Commes des Garcons, and shades by Sun Buddies.

I couldn't stop poring over the eccentric creations of Femail co-designers Camilla Carper and Janelle Abbott, who mail clothing back and forth between Washington and California, adding or removing remnants until they agree a piece is complete. The resulting pieces are bold works of art that, like the rest of the store's inventory, make you imagine you would be a more interesting person just by putting them on.

3.

TONY MOLY

234 Canal Street, Suite 112
212 625 8669
www.tonymolyny.com
Open Mon–Sun 10am–9pm

This Korean beauty store (enter at the back of New Land Plaza, via Walker St) is cuteness overload, where lip and beauty balms come in cheerful packaging, from fruits to pandas. There are also bunny-shaped perfume sticks, face soap that looks just like two boxed eggs (right down to the 'yolks'), and peeling cream concealed in a green plastic apple.

But the brand's popularity is not just about the presentation – the South Korean obsession with flawless skin has driven innovation and elevated the nation's beauty industry to a cult status that owes as much to the ritual as the results. The shop's bestsellers include Panda's Dream brightening hand cream, and sheet masks with curious ingredients such as caviar, snail and red ginseng.

Its two-storey flagship store can be found in Koreatown (35 West 32nd St).

4.

THE FAT RADISH

17 Orchard St
212 300 4053
www.thefatradishnyc.com
Open Mon–Fri 5.30pm–12am, Sat 11am–3.30pm & 5.30pm–12am, Sun 11am–3.30pm & 5.30–10pm

----

Housed in an old factory space spruced up with subway tiles, whitewash and sublime lighting, Fat Radish has a rustic interior that is pleasantly communal. The British-inspired menu is seasonal, so it changes regularly. Vegetarians are well served, with up to eight appetisers for herbivores to choose from, and a macro plate among the mains. Vegetable dishes are flavourful and surprising, unabashedly incorporating red wine, tamari, black garlic and even candied walnuts in inventive combinations.

Expect dinner items like Long Island duck breast with burnt stone fruit and onion ash, Jerusalem artichoke lasagne, or roasted brussels sprouts with plum sauce.

Make sure to leave room for that uniquely British decadence, the banoffee pie, for dessert.

Take home a cookbook or signature sweet fig candle to keep the memories alive.

LOCAL TIP

From Tony Moly, Cross Canal St to **Taiyaki NYC** (119 Baxter St) for unicorn-themed soft serve in elaborate fish-shaped waffle cones.

3.

4.

3.

5.

DIMES

49 Canal St
212 925 1300
dimesnyc.com
Open Mon–Fri 8am–11pm, Sat
9am–11pm, Sun 9am–10pm

It would have been fun to see the contractor's face when Dimes' owners, Sabrina De Sousa and Alissa Wagner, first described their vision for the interior: 'a female Japanese artist in the '60s making postmodern art in an adobe'.

The hipster crowd who gravitate to this tiny sun-splashed restaurant from the un-Manhattanly hour of 8am are rewarded with a healthy, California-inspired menu of acai bowls, nori wraps, breakfast tacos and fresh juices. Generous salads, rice bowls and sandwiches made with the house hot sauce come on at lunch, and both menus run until the kitchen closes for an hour at 4pm.

Feel-good dinner items – like salmon served on a bed of farro with fennel and beet, or Amish chicken served with chayote squash and black-eyed peas – are bountiful, and even the large plates are reasonably priced. Although the orientation is healthy, a full liquor licence means you can definitely combine your superfoods with your sense of fun. Wheatgrass margarita, anyone?

LOCAL TIP
Across the road, **Dimes Deli** (143 Division St) serves take-out versions of the restaurant menu, and has a fresh produce market.

CHINESE TUXEDO

5 Doyers St
646 895 9301
www.chinesetuxedo.com
Open Mon—Sun 6pm—12am

Having set Sydney's culinary scene on fire at Ms. G's, chef Paul Donnelly has resurfaced here, at one of a wave of new restaurants bringing the upmarket mod-Asian concept to New York. Occupying a 19th-century opera house in one of Chinatown's most storied streets, Chinese Tuxedo is the brainchild of Australian Eddy Buckingham and Chinese-American Jeff Lam.

The menu of reimagined traditional Chinese banquet dishes is not limited by a nation or a region. It offers, for example, a hot-and-sour steak tartare on homemade crab crackers, a chicken-liver pâté paired with youtiao (Chinese dough sticks), and beef 'pastrami style' served with broccoli and black bean relish.

The sunken dining room's black leather booths and the opera house's original pillars and scraped-back walls steep the room in theatrical glamour.

Reservations are recommended, but you must be a party of at least four.

At the same location is a vegan coffee shop – **The Good Sort**, open Mon—Sun 8am—6pm.

LOCAL TIP
The cheap, casual and delightfully vintage **Nom Wah Tea Parlor** (13 Doyers St) has been serving dim sum since 1920.

7.

CASA MEZCAL

86 Orchard St
212 777 2600
www.casamezcalny.com
Open Sun–Thurs 12pm–12am,
Fri–Sat 12pm–2am

The brainchild of artist Guillermo Olguin and restaurateur Ignacio Carballido, this three-storey temple to all things Oaxacan – from crafts to cuisine – is especially devoted to the artisanal elixir mezcal. This small-batch spirit, laboriously produced from slow-growing agave plants, was once ultra-niche but has more recently undergone a boom in popularity, coinciding with the passion for farm-to-table food and the rise of the craft cocktail.

Here, among the colourful paper bunting and Indigenous sculpture from central Mexico, you can drink the smoky liquor straight, sampling from an extensive range of rare mezcals that includes the house brand, Los Amantes, or visit the basement-level Botanic Lab for some innovative mixology.

Take courage and pair your drinks with taquitos de chapulin – small tacos topped with guacamole, cactus salad and crunchy grasshoppers. Or, for a more substantial meal, order the chocolatey chicken mole, made to a secret family recipe that requires more than 32 ingredients.

MR FONG'S

40 Market St
616 964 4540
www.mrfongs.com
Open Mon–Sun 5pm–4am

The founders of Mr Fong's wanted to create a bar like the ones they frequented in downtown New York 20 years ago – with a loyal crowd, understated-but-cool decor and low-cost drinks. They succeeded by securing a small space (with the help of local real estate broker Mr Fong), remote enough to test your commitment, in a quiet corner of Chinatown under Manhattan Bridge.

The bar's seven owners, who have links to the fashion, entertainment and hospitality industries, draw a fashionable crowd through word of mouth, but you'll be welcomed if you venture in. Open till 4am nightly, expect anything to manifest – from low-key sexy to a full-blown house-party vibe.

You'll find simple stirred cocktails with an Asian bent, like a salty plum old fashioned, or Szechuan peppercorn–infused tequila with watermelon, honey and lime juice. A short and slightly wonky menu of similarly inspired bar snacks is also available.

Late nights and weekends are particularly crowded – arrive early to secure one of the four burgundy leather booths.

Metrograph Cinema (7 Ludlow St) is a boutique cinema for true lovers of film. It has two screens, showing archival-quality prints as well as first-run features – many accompanied by filmmaker Q&As. It also houses a restaurant and bar inspired by the studio cafes from Hollywood's golden age, a curated candy bar, a film-themed bookshop (stocking first-edition biographies and the latest journals), and a balcony lounge in the larger theatre, with a window to see the projectionist at work in the booth.

Step into another time at the fascinating **Lower East Side Tenement Museum** (103 Orchard St), as you tour six beautifully restored apartments at 97 Orchard Street – once home to an estimated 7000 people, from more than 20 countries, between 1863 and 1935. Plan ahead as it's only accessible via guided tours, which often sell out, conducted by costumed 'residents' hailing from Sicily, Ireland and Russia. The museum also houses a well-curated New York–centric gift shop.

If you get peckish while you're exploring the Lower East Side, **Essex Street Market** (120 Essex St) houses 28 vendors selling artisanal cheese and pastries, fancy tacos and inexpensive 'pork chops for the people' – a legacy of the area's old Jewish and Italian immigrant communities. In autumn 2018, the market is set to move across Delancey to the Essex

Street Crossing development, adding 11 new vendors, plus two sit-down restaurants.

Trading since 1937, **Economy Candy** (108 Rivington St) is stocked from floor to ceiling with more than 2000 varieties of sweets, both vintage and modern brands, at discount prices. The store can get crowded, but the sense of excitement is infectious as shoppers fill their baskets with every imaginable colour of gumballs (sold individually) and M&M's (by the 2.2 kilogram bag).

The **Museum at Eldridge Street** (12 Eldridge St), which is housed in the 1887 **Eldridge Street Synagogue**, illuminates the lives of some of the Lower East Side's first Jewish residents. The synagogue, which still holds services, underwent a dazzling renovation over two decades, including the installation of a massive contemporary stained-glass window by artist Kiki Smith and architect Deborah Gans. Pay-what-you-wish tours of the synagogue are run on Mondays.

The East Village is known as the birthplace of American punk rock. It used to be a tough and gritty arts incubator, and is still Manhattan's most bohemian community. A former magnet for hippies and activists, the area retains vestiges of its counterculture past in its dive bars and poetry clubs, which now rub shoulders with cocktail lounges and vintage stores.

The neighbourhood has a diverse and affordable Asian restaurant scene, sustained by its large population of New York University students, and is the heart of Manhattan's Ukrainian and Puerto Rican populations.

 Astor Pl; 2nd Ave; 1st Ave

*Different station locations for different subway lines

Joseph C. Sauer Park

EAST 13TH STREET

EAST 11TH

EAST 12TH STREET

AVENUE B

EAST 10TH STREET

AVENUE C

NYC Parks

THE MUSEUM OF RECLAIMED URBAN SPACE

THE LOST LADY

AVENUE A

TOMPKINS SQUARE PARK

La Plaza Cultural

EAST

9th St Community Garden

Dry Dock Playground

EAST 8TH STREET

9TH

STREET

TO MAP RIGHT (VIA EAST 7TH STREET)

EAST 7TH STREET

THE WAYLAND

Firemen's Memorial Garden

6bc Botanical Garden

EAST 6TH

Green Oasis & Gilbert's Garden

LOWER EAST SIDE

EAST 5TH STREET

AVENUE C

AVENUE D

NUYORICAN POETS CAFE

EAST 4TH

El Jardin del Paraiso

STREET

Parque de Tranquilidad

STREET

Orchard Alley Garden

AVENUE B

All Peoples Garden

AVENUE D

Hamilton NYC Fish Parks Park

EAST VILLAGE

24   JUN 6016

SHOP
1 Fabulous Fanny's
2 John Derian Company
3 Verameat

EAT
4 Prune
5 Big Gay Ice Cream
6 Russ & Daughters

17

DRINK
7 Please Don't Tell
8 The Wayland

'Alamo' sculpture

ASTOR PLACE

THE PUBLIC THEATER

COOPER SQUARE

SAINT MARK'S PLACE

EAST 9TH STREET

LinkNYC

EAST 10TH STREET

LinkNYC

VERAMEAT

Theater for the New City

LinkNYC

EAST 11TH STREET

LinkNYC

Lower East Side Playground

LinkNYC

FABULOUS FANNY'S

AVENUE

STREET

The Standard Hotel East Village

EAST 7TH

LinkNYC

STREET

AVENUE

COFFEE PROJECT

2ND

LinkNYC

EAST VILLAGE

GOODNIGHT SONNY

STREET

1ST

PLEASE DON'T TELL

EAST

BOWERY

4TH

5TH

6TH STREET

LinkNYC

LinkNYC

BIG GAY ICE CREAM

A

AVENUE

STREET

STREET

JOHN DERIAN COMPANY

New York Marble Cemetery

LinkNYC

EAST

MANHATTAN

AVENUE

TO THE WAYLAND (SEE MAP LEFT)

JOHN DERIAN FURNITURE & DRY GOODS

2ND

AVENUE

ANTHOLOGY FILM ARCHIVES

New York City Marble Cemetery

3RD

STREET

LinkNYC

STREET

EAST

4TH

STREET

Liz Christy Community Garden

McKinley Playground

EAST

2ND AVENUE

First St Green Art Park

PRUNE

LinkNYC

1ST

EAST

AVENUE

3RD

2ND

STREET

o   100 m

First Park

CHRYSTIE STREET

Gatsby Hotel

Sunshine Cinema

EAST

Peretz Square

HOUSTON

2ND

N

STREET

STREET

RUSS & DAUGHTERS

STREET

STANTON

Sara D. Roosevelt Park

LinkNYC

KATZ'S DELICATESSEN

EAST

HOUSTON

STREET

LOWER EAST SIDE

FORSYTH

STREET

STREET

STREET

RIVINGTON

ORCHARD

LUDLOW

STREET

STREET

Rachel Uffner Gallery

STANTON

Suffolk Street Community Garden

ELDRIDGE

ALLEN

LinkNYC

STREET

ECONOMY CANDY

ESSEX STREET

NORFOLK

SUFFOLK STREET

RUSS & DAUGHTERS CAFE

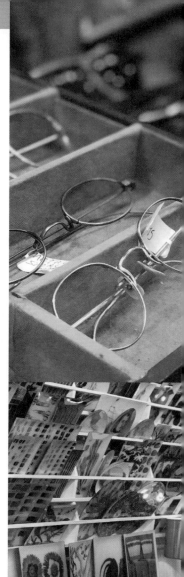

1.

FABULOUS FANNY'S

335 East 9th St
212 533 0637
Open Mon–Sun 12–8pm

Ken Finneran's collection of never-worn vintage glasses frames is considered one of the world's best. In-store is the only place you can purchase them as Finneran doesn't believe in selling frames online: 'People have to actually try them on. See what they look like, what they feel like.' Nevertheless, this pint-sized store (with an off-site inventory that numbers in the tens of thousands) has a devoted roster of international clients, including stylists and props specialists. (His wares have had a star turn in almost every Wes Anderson movie.)

Wooden dressers and glass cabinets display frames that date as far back as the 1700s – the yield of years spent scouring local and European flea markets, and acquiring deadstock frames from opticians and manufacturers. Prices start at a very modest $50. There's no in-house optician, but the assistants will refer you to several downtown experts for a quick turnaround.

2.

JOHN DERIAN COMPANY

6 East 2nd St
646 300 5575
www.johnderian.com
Open Tues–Sun 11am–7pm,
Tues–Sat (Aug), Mon–Sun (Dec)

Artist John Derian has made a name for himself with his handmade decoupage glassware, which here is piled high in a riot of antique motifs – from Valentine's cards to Nautilus shells, branches of coral, butterflies, and portraits of Native American chiefs. From paperweights and dishes to lamp bases and Christmas ornaments, it seems there's little he doesn't perceive as a potential canvas.

As well as Derian's own wares, the store showcases finds from his regular scouting trips through France, Morocco, South Asia and beyond. Come here for Cire Trudon candles from Normandy, Carrara marble fruit sculpted in Tuscany, and glossy white Astier de Villatte ceramics, handmade in Paris.

1.

2.

LOCAL TIP
Adjacent John Derian shops sell dry goods (10 East 2nd St) and furniture (8 East 2nd St) – great for covetable linens, French and American antiques, and colourful Moroccan leather goods.

3.

VERAMEAT

315 East 9th St
212 388 9045
www.verameat.com
Open Sun–Tues 12–8pm,
Wed–Sat 10am–9pm

The playful jewellery in this quintessentially East Village store make great affordable, eclectic keepsakes. Handmade designs from the Gothic imagination of Ukrainian former model Vera Balyura manage to be both uncanny and elegant. The recycled silver, brass, copper and 14-carat gold pieces are displayed on plaster hands emerging from the walls, above wooden floors stained blood-red. Hands, teeth, claws, snakes and eyes all feature heavily, along with graffiti script, and dainty rings that spell 'LOVE' and 'I [heart] NY', Robert Indiana–style.

Balyura also sells a range of clothing – including illustrated t-shirts celebrating Bill Murray or Parker Posey – limited-edition baseball caps, and quirky enamel pins of pop-culture icons, from *Gilmore Girls* and *Beetlejuice* to *Stranger Things* and *The Shining*.

PRUNE
54 East 1st St
212 677 6221
prunerestaurant.com
Open Mon–Fri 5.30–11pm,
Sat–Sun 10am–3.30pm &
5.30–11pm

- -

In a city where 'more is more', Gabrielle Hamilton's destination bistro has managed to develop a cult following in the most unexpected way – through consistently offering no-nonsense meals, full of soul and flavour.

The list of mains is concise and made up of dishes that, with the addition of some sides, can easily be shared between two – like an entire grilled branzino (European bass), or a whole spatchcocked chicken, served in a skillet. Alongside the virtuous farm-to-table ethos sits an unapologetic and very European delight in lipids: anchovy dressing, onion butter, crispy chicken-skin garnish and brussels sprouts steeped in olive oil.

Expect to line up for brunch, where the menu features no fewer than 11 bloody marys, spaghetti alla carbonara ('the Italian way to get your bacon and eggs'), giant Dutch-style pancakes and a deep-fried triple-decker sandwich.

5.

BIG GAY ICE CREAM

125 East 7th St
212 533 9333
www.biggayicecream.com
Open Sun–Wed 11am–11pm,
Thurs–Sat 11–12am

Back in 2009, Doug Quint was a freelance classical bassoonist in search of a summer job. A friend suggested operating an ice-cream truck, and in partnership with Bryan Petroff, Big Gay Ice Cream was born – later spawning this irrepressibly joyful shopfront.

If the name and rainbow-striped logo were not enough to indicate the pair don't take themselves too seriously, a mural featuring a giant unicorn, bedazzled with crystals, adorns one wall.

A simple base of vanilla or chocolate soft serve is variously dipped in chocolate and pretzels, injected with dulce de leche or coated with toasted almonds and mini-marshmallows to create the Salty Pimp, Rocky Roadhouse, Dorothy and American Globs ice-cream cones. Sundaes and milkshakes are also on offer, as well as 'Gobblers' – a wicked pie-and-ice-cream combination in a cup.

6.

RUSS & DAUGHTERS

179 East Houston St
212 475 4880
www.russanddaughters.com
Open Fri–Wed 8am–6pm,
Thurs 8am–7pm

Eastern European immigrant Joel Russ opened this 'appetising' store in 1920, taught his three daughters – Hattie, Ida and Anne – the trade and eventually made them full partners. (Anne and Hattie, then aged 92 and 100, can be seen in a 2014 documentary, *The Sturgeon Queens*, named for Russ's affectionate term for his girls).

Four generations later, the business remains in the family, turning out fish, salads and schmears for curious tourists and local customers devoted to tradition. Even if you opt for that most classic combination of smoked salmon and cream cheese on a bagel, there are eight bagels and eight types of salmon to choose from.

If you'd like a table and chair with that, head down the street to **Russ & Daughters Cafe** (127 Orchard St), modelled on the original store. This is the place to try the bulk items available from the deli – halvah scattered in pieces over sesame ice-cream, or a smoked-fish platter.

LOCAL TIP

If you're curious to see your daily caffeine habit through fresh eyes, order the nitrogen cold brew or a deconstructed latte flight at **Coffee Project** (239 East 5th St).

6.

5.

6.

7.

PLEASE DON'T TELL

113 St Marks Pl
212 614 0386
pdtnyc.com
Open Sun–Thurs 6pm–2am,
Fri–Sat 6pm–3am

Please Don't Tell (or PDT) is well and truly an open secret.

Entry is through a vintage phone booth in **Crif Dogs** – a neighbourhood mainstay known for its deep-fried frankfurters. On the other side of the booth is a compact cocktail den overlooked by taxidermied wildlife, including a bear affectionately known as Paddington – inspiration for a namesake marmalade-infused cocktail.

Meticulously crafted seasonal drinks incorporate greenmarket produce, New York–centric wines and a North-east American beer menu. They are served alongside waffle fries, 'tater tots' and anything you fancy from the Crif's kitchen next door, delivered via a hole in the wall. Try the 'Chang dog' – a collaboration with Momofuku chef David Chang, and only available inside PDT – a bacon-wrapped, deep-fried Crif dog, topped with kimchi.

The concept is pure fun, but getting a place at the table is not. The phone line opens up – and gets tied up – from 3pm.

LOCAL TIP

Other escapist East Village bars created by the same team as the Wayland are **Good Night Sonny** (134 First Ave) and nautical-themed **The Lost Lady** (171 Avenue C).

The East Village's green heart, **Tompkins Square Park** (East 10th St), has long been a site of protests and festivities, including the outdoor drag extravaganza Wigstock, the How Festival commemorating Allen Ginsberg, and the Charlie Parker Jazz Festival. A massive Halloween Dog Parade is held here, but any day of the year is great for people-watching.

Stop in to **The Museum of Reclaimed Urban Space** (155 Avenue C) to learn about the neighbourhood's radical history: the 1988 housing riots, stand-offs with police and developers over community gardens, the squatter movement, and civil disobedience by activist cyclists. You can also sign up for walking tours led by local activists and historians.

Anthology Film Archives (32 Second Ave) exhibits independent, experimental and avant-garde cinema. Check its online calendar for the constantly changing and wonderfully obscure selection.

The birthplace of late-night poetry slams, **Nuyorican Poets Cafe** (236 East 3rd St) also showcases jazz, comedy, hip-hop and other live performances to a raucous audience in an intimate space.

Katz's Delicatessen (205 East Houston St), made famous by Meg Ryan's fake orgasm in *When Harry Met Sally*, will serve you a pastrami sandwich the size of your head, without judgement.

If your taste in performance runs to the more experimental, you'll find a lot of cutting-edge arts programming in some unlikely homes. **Performance Space New York** (150 1st Ave) was established almost 40 years ago, as Performance Space 122, in an abandoned school building. From its inception, artists have collaborated on rebellious, hybrid works; mixing dance, theatre and poetry with film, music and technology to create hard-to-define pieces. **St Mark's Church-in-the-Bowery** (131 East 10th St) has supported performance and visual arts since the early 20th century – Isadora Duncan danced here, and Patti Smith read her early poetry. The place of worship, is also home to three arts organisations – **The Danspace Project**, **The Poetry Project**, and the **New York Theatre Ballet** – and hosts a range of musical performances all year. The storied **La Mama Experimental Theatre Club** (66 East 4th St) launched its mission in 1961, to foster new works by emerging local and international artists. Creators and performers who found a start here include playwright Sam Shepard, actor Robert De Niro, composer Philip Glass and comedian Amy Sedaris. Every show offers a handful of tickets for $10, but even the regular prices are kept low.

The 126-year-old **Russian and Turkish Baths** (268 East 10th St) is a first stop for many jet-lagged travellers. Alongside more conventional spa therapies – saunas, steam rooms, massage and a plunge pool – the basement bathhouse offers a coveted 'platza' treatment. Lie down in the Russian Room and be whipped with a broom made from fresh oak leaves, sopping with olive oil soap. If that sounds too intense, rejuvenate with a salt scrub or mud treatment, with materials imported from the Dead Sea.

Map

STAR STRUCK VINTAGE

WEST 11TH STREET

GREENWICH AVENUE

WEST 10TH STREET

6TH AVENUE

WEST 10TH AVENUE

Jefferson Market Library

Jefferson Market Garden

9TH STREET (PATH)

CHRISTOPHER STREET

WEST 8TH STREET

LOMOGRAPHY

GOODS FOR THE STUDY

WAVERLY AVENUE

6TH AVENUE

PLACE

Washington Square Hotel

TO
MAP RIGHT
(VIA 6TH AVENUE)

Washington Square Park

NYC Parks

GREENWICH VILLAGE

Greenwich Village, once the epicentre of bohemian life in Manhattan and home to poets, writers, beatniks, actors and musicians, is still a vibrant hive of entertainment and creativity. You'll find some of the city's best comedy shows, bars and clubs, making the area a must-see.

Originally made up of stately terraces (around picturesque 10th Street) and impoverished tenements around Bleecker (complete with genuine Mafia godfathers), 'the Village' has been home to Edgar Allen Poe, Jack Kerouac, Allen Ginsberg, Jackson Pollock, Andy Warhol, Patti Smith, Jimi Hendrix and Bob Dylan.

West 4th St–Washington Sq; Houston St; Christopher St
*Different station locations for different subway lines

24   JUN 80T6

SHOP
1 Star Struck Vintage
2 Goods for the Study
3 Generation Records
EAT
4 Minetta Tavern
5 Miss Lily's

EAT & DRINK
6 Mermaid Inn Oyster Bar
DRINK
7 Blue Note Jazz Club
8 Comedy Cellar

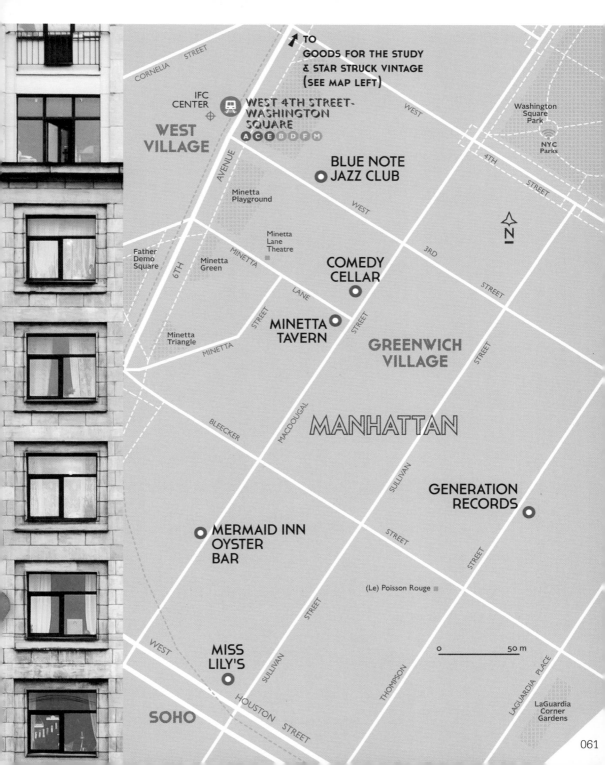

TO
**GOODS FOR THE STUDY
& STAR STRUCK VINTAGE**
(SEE MAP LEFT)

IFC
CENTER

**WEST 4TH STREET-
WASHINGTON
SQUARE**
Ⓐ Ⓒ Ⓔ Ⓑ Ⓓ Ⓕ Ⓜ

WEST

CORNELIA   STREET

**WEST
VILLAGE**

Washington
Square
Park

NYC
Parks

Minetta
Playground

**BLUE NOTE
JAZZ CLUB**

WEST

4TH   STREET

N

AVENUE

Minetta
Lane
Theatre

Father
Demo
Square

Minetta
Green

MINETTA

**COMEDY
CELLAR**

3RD

6TH

LANE

STREET

STREET

Minetta
Triangle

**MINETTA
TAVERN**

MINETTA

STREET

**GREENWICH
VILLAGE**

STREET

BLEECKER

MACDOUGAL

MANHATTAN

SULLIVAN

**GENERATION
RECORDS**

STREET

**MERMAID INN
OYSTER
BAR**

STREET

STREET

STREET

(Le) Poisson Rouge

STREET

WEST

**MISS
LILY'S**

SULLIVAN

o ————————— 50 m

THOMPSON

LAGUARDIA PLACE

LaGuardia
Corner
Gardens

SOHO

HOUSTON   STREET

1.

STAR STRUCK VINTAGE
47 Greenwich Ave
212 691 5357
www.starstruckvintage.com
Open Mon–Sat 11am-8pm,
Sun 12–7pm

The Village has always been the backdrop for counterculture cool, so when you're looking for the best range of rock 'n' roll chic, disco throwbacks and leather jackets, you're sure to find gold within the very streets where punk, folk and disco first began.

Star Struck Vintage is a thrift shop bursting at the seams with rare finds. Its tightly overflowing racks are cluttered and disorganised, which will lead you on a treasure hunt through decades and styles. There's a definite edge to the range, with a large collection of vintage gig shirts dating back to the '70s and rack upon rack of well-worn denim. Try on flapper hats from the early 20th century, old ball gowns, vintage furs (though avoid the back wall if that offends), belt buckles and Boy Scout uniforms. Being in the Village, you may even uncover some genuine designer-label steals, but be prepared to pay a pretty penny for some of the more collectable finds.

GOODS FOR THE STUDY

50 West 8th St
212 674 4400
www.goodsforthestudy.
mcnallyjacksonstore.com
Open Mon–Sun 10am–8pm

With many of us never glancing up from our phone or computer screen, the feelings evoked by handwritten words have become something to be treasured. Goods For the Study has come to the rescue of this dying art. In a setting reminiscent of a late 19th-century English corner store, with accents of walnut, gold and warm ambient lighting, walls of colourful pens in labelled jars sit adjacent to orderly tables of neatly arranged notepads and journals. Owned by indie bookstore outfit McNally Jackson (see p. 028), this artful stationer is a cosy haven for every writer or paper lover.

Take some time to browse the large range of unique and designer greeting cards with witty slogans and whimsical imagery, limited-edition prints, wrapping paper and stylish gifts, all the while listening to cool tunes, courtesy of the store's tasteful and incredibly hip staffers.

3.

GENERATION RECORDS
210 Thompson St
212 254 1100
www.generationrecordsnyc.com/
generation/generation.html
Open Sun–Thurs 12–9pm,
Fri–Sat 12–10pm

There was a time when Greenwich Village had a thriving record store scene with landmark shops like Bleecker Street Records and Rebel Rebel. Generation Records is one of the last and a haven for vinyl junkies. Its focus is on independent music and heavier genres like punk, hardcore and metal, though you may be surprised by the range of older jazz, blues and funk records waiting to be discovered.

The street level is overflowing with the latest CDs and DVDs but the shellac is downstairs. The dimly lit basement provides the perfect ambience for foraging through crates of LPs, 78s and 45s. Browse racks of band t-shirts, gig posters and a killer collection of vintage toys. Periodically the basement's tiny stage hosts underground gigs by influential local acts.

4.

MINETTA TAVERN
113 MacDougal St
212 475 3850
www.minettatavernny.com
Open Sun–Wed
5.30pm–12am, Thurs–Sat
5.30pm –1am (dinner), Wed–
Fri 12–3pm, Sat–Sun 11am–
3pm (lunch)

Since the 1930s, this dimly lit French bistro has been a Village hotspot and in recent years, it has undergone a reinvention that has made it a must-visit for foodies. With curtains drawn and shades closed, its decor remains a mystery to passersby, offering a quiet space for a date night or dalliance. It's what attracts celebrities, so be sure to dress the part. Between courses, it's fun to peruse the floor-to-ceiling framed photos of past guests dating back to the golden age of cinema. The real star is the Black Label Burger, which has earned the Minetta Tavern its Michelin Star. With its own secret blend of beef, marrow and caramelised onions, the burger is so luxurious you'll feel guilty for using your fingers. Booking ahead is recommended. With only 70 seats, this hotspot has a lengthy wait list and comes with a premium price tag.

LOCAL TIP

During summer months, take the Rock 'n' Roll walking tour, led by John Joseph, lead singer of legendary NY hardcore punk outfit The Cro-Mags to discover the area's rich musical history. Ask for details at Generation Records.

4.

3.

4.

5.

MISS LILY'S

132 West Houston St
212 812 1482
www.misslilys.com
Open Mon–Wed
11.30am–11.30pm, Thurs–Fri
11.30–12.30am, Sat–Sun
11–12.30am

Seinfeld character George Costanza immortalised the line, 'Well, the Jerk Store called, and they're running out of you'. Luckily Miss Lily's never runs out of its famous jerk chicken. The vibe is friendly and laidback, right in sync with the food that is warming, rich and comforting. Established in 2011, this restaurant-come-juice-bar-come-rum-bar-come-reggae-radio-station has developed quite a cult following (just like its East Village brother) so reservations are recommended.

Step inside to decor that is as brash and loud as the speaker decals on the walls that transport you to a local Jamaican street party, minus the barbecue smoke. Try the oxtail stew with a side of rice and beans, or the half a blackened chicken with its fragrant array of jerk spices. Go during happy hour to try Lily's Punch (made from soju, fresh orange, passionfruit and pineapple), or a freshly squeezed Melvin's Juice.

6.

MERMAID INN OYSTER BAR

79 MacDougal St
www.themermaidnyc.com
Open Mon 5–10pm, Tues–Fri 5–10.30pm, Sat 4–10.30pm, Sun 4–10pm

----

Mermaid Inn brings the whitewashed New England fishing shack to life with some of the region's best seafood. The white weatherboard interior is stylishly accented with framed prints and old black and white photos of quaint seaside scenes.

This local hotspot dishes up tasty oysters, the freshest of chowders and seasonal lobster specials. But it's during happy hours that it truly shines. Treat yourself to discounted cocktails like the Dark and Stormy, made with a zesty local ginger beer, or their Mermaid Mary, and load up on $1 oysters, shrimp corndogs and tuna tartare taquitos. If you still have room, try one of the mains like the British-style crispy cod and chips. Book ahead via their website. The place fills up quickly so be there on opening time or leave your phone number and get called when a space opens for you. If you love seafood, it's always worth the wait.

5.

6.

LOCAL TIP
Drop into **Dante** (71–81 MacDougal St) next door to the Mermaid Inn. An established favourite, it offers a dimly lit atmosphere in which you can enjoy 12 flavours of Negroni, served by fashionably dressed bartenders.

7.

BLUE NOTE JAZZ CLUB

131 West 3rd St
212 475 8592
www.bluenote.net
Open Mon–Sun 6pm–12am

There's no shortage of older, goatee-stroking bohemians and saxophone-carrying jazz cats coming and going from this iconic club. Since 1981, the Blue Note has been celebrating, promoting, supporting and exporting the best of the jazz world. Early guests included Dizzy Gillespie, Oscar Peterson and Ray Charles, and the club still hosts the crème de la crème of modern jazz greats like Chris Botti, Chick Corea, Jools Holland, Victor Wooten and John Scofield.

The decor is preserved in a time capsule with dated vinyl, luminous surfaces and a neon rendering of the Manhattan skyline, but so much of the music performed here is timeless, so it's perfectly fitting. And it's the music that keeps the crowds gathering outside long before each set. While the drinks menu is quite expensive and the cocktail list can only be described as a jazz standard, you'll get your money's worth the moment the main act hits its opening chord. Book tickets in advance via the website. The dress code is smart casual.

LOCAL TIP
For a taste of great live jazz washed down with a mimosa or bloody mary, the Blue Note hosts jazz brunches on Sundays at 12.30pm and 2.30pm. Reservations recommended.

COMEDY CELLAR
117 MacDougal St
212 254 3480
www.comedycellar.com
Open Mon–Sun with shows at
7.30pm, 9.30pm and 11pm

The funniest part about a show at the Comedy Cellar is that you never know who's going to drop by to try out their latest jokes. Comedy greats from Jerry Seinfeld to Robin Williams to the new guard like Judah Friedlander have trod the boards and it is renowned for impromptu performances by comedy royalty.

The venue is disarmingly humble. Descend the steps below its flashing sign and simple whiteboard announcing the nightly lineup, and enter its iconic red brick basement, which will surprise you with its intimacy. The close quarters will leave you and the other audience members in delicious anticipation of who'll be picked out for special attention by the stand-up comedian. There's a two-drink minimum, but you will probably need them.

Washington Square Park
(bordering 5th Ave, Waverly Pl, West 4th St and MacDougal St) has had a long and varied history, from burial ground to the site of beatnik protests. It is the beating heart of the village, where you'll experience buskers playing a grand piano under the George Washington Arch (where artist Marcel Duchamp and painter John Sloan climbed to the top and tried to secede the Village from the rest of America in 1917), challenge chess sharks in the south-west corner, meet the Pigeon Man and his flocks of pigeons, and in the warmer months see kids playing in its iconic fountain. The park is bordered by New York University (NYU) buildings on all sides, with classic terraces home to faculties, the Judson Memorial Church (a village icon and art space on its south side) and Washington Square West, where Eleanor Roosevelt lived at No. 29 from 1942–49.

Film buffs should stop by the **Film Forum** (209 West Houston St) to catch a classic or independent release. For a different type of celluloid, explore the **Lomography store** (West 8th St) where affordable vintage Russian film cameras have been re-created for the Instagram generation.

West 8th Street also offers some hidden treasures. Although not open to the public, **Electric Lady Studios** (52 West 8th St), was owned and opened by Jimi Hendrix in 1970 and is where iconic albums like ACDC's 'Back in Black', Led Zeppelin's 'Houses of the Holy', Prince's 'Graffiti Bridge' and David Bowie's 'Young

Americans' were recorded. **Stumptown Coffee** (30 West 8th St) is the headquarters for this local grind that can be found at the most hip cafes across the city. Its walls are lined with books written by those who have called the Village home.

Head up MacDougal Street, passing **MacDougal Alley** with its former horse stables and cobbled streets, to West 3rd and Bleecker and delve further into the area's history. **Caffe Reggio** (119 MacDougal St) is one of the oldest tenants in the area, serving up coffee to the local Italian migrant population that live in the tenements around Minetta Lane. It has been featured in films like *Godfather 2* and delivers some fine cannoli. **Cafe Wha?** (115 MacDougal St) is where Jimi

Hendrix was discovered and acts as diverse as Richard Pryor and Bob Dylan regularly performed. Other iconic venues that have long disappeared but that are immortalised in music history include San Remo Cafe and the Gaslight Cafe.

For live music, check out the **Bitter End** (147 Bleecker St), where '60s bands like Jefferson Airplane and Peter, Paul and Mary started; the **Red Lion** (151 Bleecker St) for quality pub cover bands; or head across the road to **Le Poisson Rouge** (158 Bleecker St), in the space of the Old Village Gate (another famed venue from the '60s – its original hoarding is preserved above the CVS signage on the corner of Bleecker and Thompson) for current pop acts and avant-garde performances.

Arguably Manhattan's most picturesque neighbourhood, the West Village, with its tree-lined streets and 19th-century townhouses, feels like a movie-set version of idealised New York. Strolling the mostl residential area reveals charming cafes and boutiques, cosy bars, peaceful parks and restaurants of long standing.

This compact precinct has been the site of several significant social movements, including the fight for housing preservation and the gay liberation movement, which in 1969 galvanised around a series of demonstrations outside the Stonewall Inn (see p. 082).

 Christopher St; 14th St; West 4th St–Washington Sq

*Different station locations for different subway lines

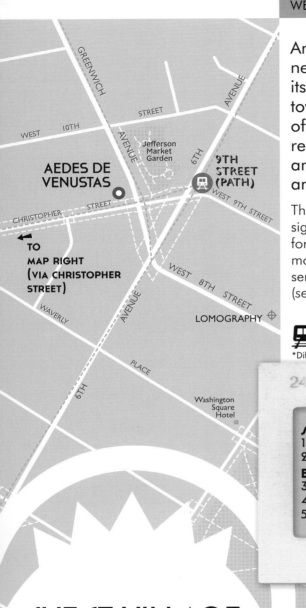

GREENWICH STREET

AVENUE

STREET

WEST 10TH

6TH

Jefferson Market Garden

AEDES DE VENUSTAS

9TH STREET (PATH)

CHRISTOPHER STREET

WEST 9TH STREET

← TO MAP RIGHT (VIA CHRISTOPHER STREET)

AVENUE

WEST 8TH STREET

LOMOGRAPHY

WAVERLY

PLACE

6TH

Washington Square Hotel

WEST VILLAGE

24   JUN 6076

SHOP
1 AEDES DE VENUSTAS
2 MADAME MATOVU
EAT
3 BUVETTE
4 THE SPOTTED PIG
5 THE ELK

17

DRINK
6 LITTLE BRANCH
7 EMPLOYEES ONLY

BANK STREET

Bleecker Playground

WEST 11TH STREET

BLEECKER STREET

WEST 11TH STREET

WEST STREET

STREET

4TH STREET

PERRY STREET

SOUTH

O THE SPOTTED PIG

Carrie Bradshaw apartment

GREENWICH STREET

WEST 11TH STREET

MANHATTAN

PERRY STREET

STREET

7TH AVENUE

TO AEDES DE VENUSTAS (SEE MAP LEFT) →

CHARLES STREET

CHARLES STREET

STREET

O THE ELK

HUDSON STREET

10TH STREET

STREET

CHRISTOPHER STREET-SHERIDAN SQUARE

STONEWALL INN

⊕

GAY LIBERATION MONUMENT

⊕

WEST STREET

O MADAME MATOVU

EMPLOYEES O ONLY

CHRISTOPHER STREET

1 🚇

Christopher Park

STREET

CHRISTOPHER STREET (PATH)

🚇

BEDFORD STREET

GROVE STREET

O BUVETTE

STREET

WEST VILLAGE

WEST 4TH STREET

📶 LinkNYC

STREET

BARROW STREET

BLEECKER STREET

JONES STREET

WEST 4TH STREET-WASHINGTON SQUARE

A C E B D F M

BARROW STREET

📶 LinkNYC

STREET

SOUTH AVENUE

IFC CENTER

🚇

0 ___ 100 m

MORTON STREET

STREET

LEROY STREET

STREET

Father Demo Square

Minetta Lane Theatre

LEROY

📶 LinkNYC

LITTLE BRANCH

STREET

HUDSON STREET

7TH

⇧ N

STREET

James J Walker Park

NYC Parks

CARMINE STREET

GREENWICH VILLAGE

STREET

6TH AVENUE

CLARKSON STREET

DOWNING STREET

HOUSTON STREET

1 🚇

FILM FORUM

MacDougal-Sullivan Gardens Historic District

WEST HOUSTON STREET

STREET ⊕

William E Passannante Ballfield

✉

073

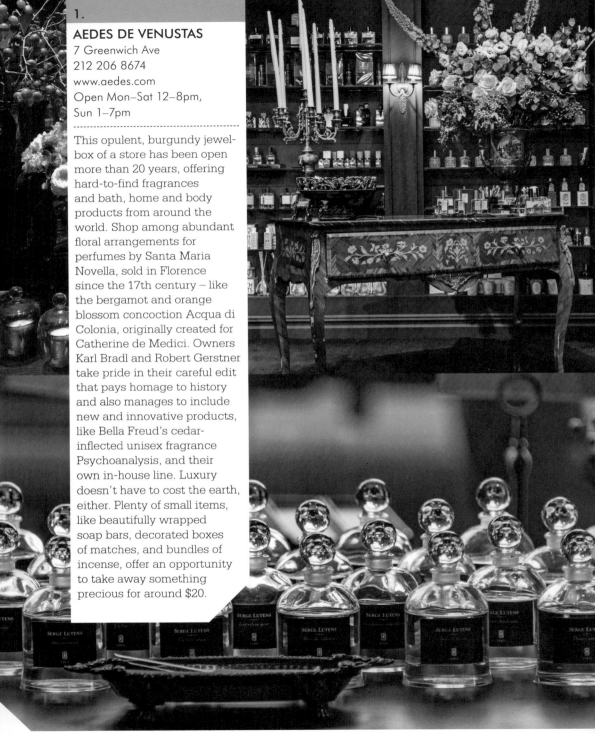

1.

AEDES DE VENUSTAS

7 Greenwich Ave
212 206 8674
www.aedes.com
Open Mon–Sat 12–8pm,
Sun 1–7pm

This opulent, burgundy jewel-box of a store has been open more than 20 years, offering hard-to-find fragrances and bath, home and body products from around the world. Shop among abundant floral arrangements for perfumes by Santa Maria Novella, sold in Florence since the 17th century – like the bergamot and orange blossom concoction Acqua di Colonia, originally created for Catherine de Medici. Owners Karl Bradl and Robert Gerstner take pride in their careful edit that pays homage to history and also manages to include new and innovative products, like Bella Freud's cedar-inflected unisex fragrance Psychoanalysis, and their own in-house line. Luxury doesn't have to cost the earth, either. Plenty of small items, like beautifully wrapped soap bars, decorated boxes of matches, and bundles of incense, offer an opportunity to take away something precious for around $20.

MADAME MATOVU
240 West 10th St
212 255 2811
Open Tues–Sat 12–7pm,
Sun 12–5.30pm

Born in Uganda to diplomat parents, Rosemary Wettenhall inherited both worldliness and charm, which she uses to advantage in this diminutive vintage fashion and accessories boutique. Under the watchful eye of the store's logo – a French Revolutionary woman in a bold head-wrap and pearls – the store is brimming with Wettenhall's finds from around the world, particularly France and Italy. Jumbled together, flea-market style, are 1950s evening dresses, sequinned jackets and one-of-a-kind belts and handbags, displayed alongside sparkling costume jewellery and homewares. The mix runs from high-end labels (Gucci, Chanel, YSL) to Hawaiian tourist dresses from the 1960s and chunky rhinestone necklaces, but all of it reflects Wettenhall's eclectic and ultra-feminine taste. Ask to see inside the 'secret' cabinet, which holds delicate beaded clutches and other precious, big-ticket items. Not that she is elitist about labels – she advocates strongly for the confident combination of a t-shirt with Chanel couture, giving new personality to old items.

3.

BUVETTE
42 Grove St
212 255 3590
https://ilovebuvette.com
Open Mon–Fri 7–2am,
Sat–Sun 8–2am

A buvette is a place to eat or drink at any time of the day, and that is just what is on offer here, with small plates served at small tables in a diminutive room styled with flea market finds.

Under owner-chef Jody Williams, breakfast standouts include the classic croque monsieur with ham and gruyère (also served at lunchtime), and any of the plates featuring smooth scrambled eggs steamed with the frother of an espresso machine.

At dinnertime, the servings are shrunk to meet the limitations of the space but are packed with flavour. Anchoiade tartinette spread with generous slabs of butter and salty anchovies; and a tiny crock filled with rich coq au vin and a serve of julienned carrots tossed in lemon juice can be happily shared between two.

There are no reservations so take your chances on getting a table, but even a late-night cocktail at the beautiful marble bar is sufficient to soak up the cosy Gallic ambience and leave feeling romanced.

4.

THE SPOTTED PIG
314 West 11th St
212 620 0393
www.thespottedpig.com
Open Mon–Fri 12pm–2am,
Sat–Sun 11–2am

The kitchen of this wildly popular bi-level gatropub has been turning out seasonal British and Italian food amid a buzzy social scene since 2004.

Under pedigreed owner-chef April Bloomfield (London's River Cafe, Chez Panisse), the star of the show remains the chargrilled burger – heaped with potent roquefort cheese and served with a sprawling pile of shoestring fries flavoured with rosemary and garlic. Other staples that have achieved legendary status include gnocchi-like ricotta gnudi with brown butter and crisped sage leaves, a crispy pig's ear salad with a lemony caper dressing, and the flourless chocolate cake.

After all these years, the Spotted Pig remains a walk-in only venue, and getting a table for dinner – even with two in-house bars – can test your patience. Come instead for a weekday lunch, when there is hardly ever a wait, and indulge in the serious beer and wine lists that confer its status with foodies.

3.

4.

4.

4.

3.

4.

5.

THE ELK

128 Charles St
212 933 4780
www.theelknyc.com
Open Mon–Fri 7am–7pm,
Sat–Sun 8am–7pm

This compact cafe and 'general store' overlooks a quiet side street, and sells an eclectic little selection of locally made lifestyle goods alongside healthy breakfasts and lunches. It was founded by former fashion buyer Claire Chan, and everything is 'just so', from the bright space and raw wood interiors to the single-origin pour-over coffees and cage-free local eggs.

Browse among goods made in and near New York, including Izola candles, 1940s-era Chemex coffee makers, coffee by Brooklyn roasters Parlor, and eco-friendly hand soap from Williamsburg provedore Common Good.

Select between the laptop bar and the designated laptop-free tables, and order an egg sandwich made with Sullivan Street Bakery's potato panino, or the nourishing market rice bowl. If seating is hard to come by, choose a Balthazar or Ovenly treat from the glass pastry-case and take your coffee a couple of blocks west to the large park on Pier 45, part of the impressive Hudson River Greenway.

6.

LITTLE BRANCH

20 7th Ave South
212 929 4360
Open Mon–Sat 7pm–3am,
Sun 7pm–2am

By day, this speakeasy hides in plain sight in an ugly, bunker-like apartment building. When it opens for business at 7pm, the bouncer – and sometimes a short line – will tip you off that something appealing is being cooked up below stairs.

Once inside, you'll be led down to the basement bar, small and candlelit, where jazz is playing (often live) and swanky bartenders will serve you a strong, classic cocktail over ice chipped from blocks.

Serious drinks aficionados will recognise the legacy of late cocktail proponent Sasha Petraske, whose other establishments included Milk & Honey, on the Lower East Side, the Varnish in Los Angeles, and the Everleigh in Melbourne. Petraske was also a champion of the 'bartender's choice', whereby you surrender to the expertise of the highly skilled staff, who only need a hint of your likes and dislikes to conjure a customised drink.

The bar takes cash only and there's no food menu – just complimentary nuts and pretzels, yielding to the expertly crafted cocktails and friendly chatter.

5.

5.

6.

7.

EMPLOYEES ONLY

510 Hudson St
212 242 3021
www.employeesonlynyc.com
Open Mon–Sun 6pm–4am

If you make it to closing time (4am) here, expect to be dished out a bowl of homemade chicken soup. It's part of the general bonhomie of this longstanding 'secret' nightspot, which you access via a fortune-telling business. The vibe is Golden Age, with Art Deco features throughout, white-jacketed bar staff, and an elevated dining room featuring a wrap-around banquette and overhead luggage racks.

All aboard for craft cocktails, including several that were pioneered here, like the Amelía (a potpourri of vodka and St-Germain shaken with pureed blackberries and lemon juice). A 'fancy cocktails' menu raises the stakes a notch, introducing jalapeño-infused Chartreuse, Hellfire bitters and mezcal into the ingredients list.

Reservations are only taken for dinner, with a late-night menu served daily from midnight until 3.30am. In winter, the fireplace is lit.

John Coltrane, Miles Davis and Bill Evans have all graced the stage at the **Village Vanguard** (178 7th Ave South), which has been devoted to an all-jazz program since 1957, and where the 16-piece Vanguard Jazz Orchestra has played a Monday-night slot since 1966.

Raise a glass to a piece of history at the **Stonewall Inn** (53 Christopher St) – a gay bar and the site of the Stonewall Riots of 1969, which launched the gay rights movement in the United States. Across the street in **Christopher Park** is George Segal's **Gay Liberation** monument, installed in 1992, depicting two standing and two seated figures.

Across the road from Christopher Park, gather round the piano at legendary bar **Marie's Crisis** (59 Grove St) for heartfelt show-tunes singalongs.

Actors and directors often appear for Q&As on opening nights at the **IFC Center** (323 6th Ave) – a five-screen art-house cinema showing new-release independent and foreign films, documentaries, classics and midnight cult screenings.

Fans of 1990s TV can snap a photo of themselves outside the apartment of Sex and the City's Carrie Bradshaw (66 Perry St), or get nostalgic at the Friends building (90 Bedford St).

Join a nature walk (Christopher Street Fountain) or take a trapeze class (Pier 40) in **Hudson River Park** – a 220 hectare (543 acre) riverside park and estuarine sanctuary that runs all the way north to West 59th Street.

Garden enthusiasts and those in search of tranquillity should visit the beautifully landscaped grounds of the **Church of St Luke in the Fields** (487 Hudson St) – more than 2700 square metres (29,062 square feet) of walks and lawns, in five sections, featuring a rose garden, rare hybrids and native American flora.

For homesick Brits and Anglophiles, visit grocery store **Myers of Keswick** (634 Hudson St) to pick up British food favourites, or try English comfort-food cafe **Tea & Sympathy** (108 Greenwich Ave) for dishes like Bangers and Mash and Sticky Date Pudding.

The trendy Meatpacking District, once the site of slaughterhouses and packing plants, is home to the **Whitney Museum of American Art** (see p. 094), and its cobbled streets brim with clubs, restaurants, designer boutiques and luxury hotels. It is the start of the **High Line** (see p. 094) – a brilliant elevated park – and you can walk all the way to the adjacent art district, Chelsea.

The formerly industrial Chelsea has given way to residences and exhibition spaces, as well as breathtaking high-rises by architecture superstars. Chelsea is a bastion of the LGBTQI community, with a lively gay bar scene.

14th St; 23rd St

*Different station locations for different subway lines

Map

Magnet Theater

Holiday Inn Express New York City Chelsea

LinkNYC

LinkNYC

WEST 28TH STREET

WEST 27TH STREET

28TH STREET

Museum at the Fashion Institute of Technology

TO MAP RIGHT (VIA WEST 26TH STREET)

FLOWER DISTRICT

SID GOLD'S REQUEST ROOM

LinkNYC

LinkNYC

WEST 24TH

LinkNYC

Senton Hotel

LinkNYC

Chelsea Savoy Hotel

23RD STREET

The Townhouse Inn of Chelsea

LinkNYC

Hotel Henri

23RD STREET

WEST 31ST STREET

WEST 30TH STREET

WEST 29TH STREET

WEST 26TH

WEST 25TH

WEST 22ND

WEST 21ST STREET

WEST 20TH STREET

WEST 19TH STREET

WEST 23RD

MEATPACKING DISTRICT & CHELSEA

24   JUN 8016

SHOP
1 PRINTED MATTER
2 STORY

SHOP & EAT
3 CHELSEA MARKET/ ARTISTS & FLEAS

17

EAT
4 SANTINA
5 EMPIRE DINER
6 MOMOFUKU NISHI

DRINK
7 SID GOLD'S REQUEST ROOM
8 TOP OF THE STANDARD

PRINTED
MATTER

LinkNYC

High Line
stair access

WEST 29TH STREET

McKittrick
Hotel

WEST 28TH STREET

HIGH LINE

WEST 24TH STREET

11TH AVENUE

WEST 25TH STREET

High Line
stair access

10TH STREET

NYC
Parks

Chelsea
Park

Chelsea
Waterside
Park

WEST 26TH STREET

WEST 24TH STREET

MANHATTAN

CHELSEA
PIERS

WEST 23RD STREET

High Line
stair & elevator
access

STREET

9TH

TO
SID GOLD'S
REQUEST ROOM
(SEE MAP LEFT)

Penn
South
Playground

22ND

NYC
Parks

EMPIRE
DINER

WEST 21ST STREET

Clement
Clarke
Moore
Park

WEST 23RD
STREET

CHELSEA

23RD
STREET

C E

HIGH LINE

10TH AVENUE

High Line
stair access

WEST 20TH STREET

21ST STREET

The GEM
Hotel

LinkNYC

STORY

WEST STREET

AVENUE

MOMOFUKU
NISHI

High Line
stair access

10TH

11TH

Northern
Spur
Preserve

10th Avenue
Square &
overlook

High Line
stair & elevator
access

WEST 19TH STREET

Linda Gross
Theater

LinkNYC

9TH STREET

WEST 18TH STREET

ARTISTS
& FLEAS

Diller-Von Furstenberg
sundeck &
water feature

THE
JOYCE
THEATER

LinkNYC

Maritime
Hotel

WEST 17TH STREET

High Line
stair & elevator
access

CHELSEA
MARKET

WEST 14TH STREET

Doctor
Gertrude B Kelly
Playground

LinkNYC

16TH STREET

8TH AVENUE

0   100 m

LinkNYC

TOP OF THE
STANDARD

WEST 13TH STREET

15TH STREET

N

WEST
VILLAGE

14TH STREET-
8TH AVENUE
A C E L

SANTINA

LinkNYC

WHITNEY
MUSEUM
OF AMERICAN
ART

GANSEVOORT STREET

Corporal
John A Seravalli
Playground

Jackson
Square
Park

14TH
STREET

1 2 3

085

1.

PRINTED MATTER
231 11th Ave
212 925 0325
www.printedmatter.org
Open Mon–Wed 11am–7pm,
Thurs–Fri, 11am–8pm, Sat
11am–7pm, Sun 12–6pm

Housed in an abandoned
train terminal, Printed
Matter trades in a weird and
wonderful range of limited
edition books and zines
made by artists, numbering
in the thousands, more than
40 years after it was founded
by artist Sol LeWitt and
critic Lucy Lippard. You can
souvenir something special:
the store aims to make its
books-as-art affordable to
everyone, with most works
between $5 and $50, with the
exception of a handful of rare
and special interest works.
If you're seeking a particular
book, it's better to search the
store's continuously updated
online database before
visiting. You can also buy
art periodicals, postcards,
posters and apparel,
including Yoko Ono's 'breast
button', Kittens Against
Trump tote bags, and text
artist Eve Fowler's letterpress
posters celebrating the poetry
of Gertrude Stein. There is
also a gallery space, which is
refreshed monthly, displaying
archival material, or newly
minted reprints and limited
editions for sale.

2.

STORY
144 10th Ave
212 242 4853
www.thisisstory.com
Open Tues–Wed 11am–7pm,
Thurs 11am–8pm, Fri–Sat
11am–7pm

Blink and you might miss the
latest version of this concept
store, which mirrors the
editorial style of a magazine
by completely refreshing
the decor and merchandise
every three to eight weeks.
Former marketing consultant
Rachel Schechtman takes
an overarching theme
and curates a collection of
products – from gadgets to
fashion – mixing yet-to-be
discovered vendors with
famous brands, completely
redesigning the store to
match. Narratives so far
have been as diverse as Love
Story, Disrupt, Fresh, New
York, as well as an annual
holiday edition at the end
of the year, with the work of
finding fresh and obscure
brands done for you. The
space also operates as a
cultural hub, hosting Q&As
with designers and hundreds
of classes, from pilates and
laser-cutting to pasta-making
and mixology.

2.

1.

3.

CHELSEA MARKET/ ARTISTS & FLEAS

75 9th Ave
212 652 2121
www.chelseamarket.com
Open Mon–Sat 7am–9pm,
Sun 8am–8pm

Gather supplies from this huge indoor marketplace, housed in a former biscuit factory, and take a picnic to the High Line. More than 30 food vendors and retailers share the converted warehouses with a large outpost of the **Artists & Fleas** market, offering artwork, jewellery and new and vintage fashion. Head to the 20-seat sushi bar at **The Lobster Place** for a raw seafood breakfast inspired by Tokyo's Tsukiji fish market, or a Nutella crepe from **Bar Suzette**. A discreet internal hallway from **Los Tacos No. 1** – one of the city's best taquerias – leads down to **Los Mariscos**; a seafood spin-off that offers a raw bar, beer and cocktails at whitewashed picnic tables, as well as delicious fish tacos made from family recipes.

A favourite brunch item is delicious and fortifying shakshuka (baked eggs in a spicy tomato stew with fresh pita), served all day at **Dizengoff**, along with Israeli-style frozen mint lemonade or Israeli wines by the glass.

4.

SANTINA

820 Washington St
www.santinanyc.com
Open Sun–Tues 10am–10pm,
Wed–Sat 10–12am

A casually glamorous seaside vibe abounds within this restaurant devoted to Italian coastal cuisine, touchingly named for chef Mario Carbone's grandmother. The Renzo Piano-designed glass cube is illuminated by extravagant custom-made Venetian Murano glass chandeliers and houses hand-painted plates from Salerno, blue banquette seating and wait staff wearing blue polo shirts. Specialties include whole porgies (sea bream) and the cecina – a chickpea flour pancake that pairs with toppings such as spicy tuna tartare or avocado and almond pesto. Rice dishes get their own menu section, including the beautifully simple broccoli and pecorino, and the more indulgent guanciale (pork jowl) and pepper. The cocktails feature a range of summery ingredients; and after an Amalfi Gold – concocted from bourbon, orange, ginger and peach – the nearby Hudson River can take on a decidedly Mediterranean hue. For a special meal before or after taking in the Whitney or the High Line, book ahead.

3.

4.

4.

3.

3.

4.

5.

EMPIRE DINER

210 10th Ave
212 335 2277
www.empire-diner.com
Open Mon–Sun 8–1am

This freestanding retro diner, built in 1946, is a cult classic, featured on the cover of Tom Waits' *Asylum Years* album, and in films including *Home Alone 2*, *Men in Black 2*, and Woody Allen's black-and-white ode to the city, *Manhattan*. But while the building is beloved, the culinary experience suffered some false starts over the years. That is, until 2017, when chef John DeLucie (**Bedford & Co.**) and the team behind local 24/7 mainstay **Cafeteria** (119 7th Ave), refurbed the interior with soft leather banquettes and pale wood, and brought fresh interpretations of American classics. Fried chicken gets a sourdough pretzel crust, hanger steak is served with a black truffle vinaigrette, and pigs in a blanket feature confit pork and pickled cabbage. The refined diner fare remains comforting, and the warm interiors have proved a hit with art lovers fortifying themselves for a Chelsea gallery-crawl.

MOMOFUKU NISHI
232 8th Ave
646 518 1919
nishi.momofuku.com
Open Mon–Sun 12–3pm &
5.30–11pm

This newly renovated
and reopened Italian
restaurant has an Asian-
fusion provenance under
its innovators, Momofuku
impresario David Chang and
chef Joshua Pinsky. Bucatini
cacio et pepe, for example,
is turned vegan by replacing
cheese with chickpea miso; a
whole fried lobster is served
on noodles with garlic and
chilli; crispy fried shrimp
grace the appetisers; and
pork ribs are served with a
sweet and sour garlic sauce.
Then there's the Impossible
Burger, served three ways
on the lunch menu. The
invention of a Silicon Valley
start-up, it warranted its own
profile in *Wired* magazine as
'the fake meat that "bleeds"',
with a patty entirely made
of plants, that sizzles, smells
and tastes as if it were crafted
from the finest beef. A limited
number of this eco-friendly
oddity of Californian food
science are available daily
on a first-come, first-served
basis, so booking for a lunch
sitting is advised.

7.

SID GOLD'S REQUEST ROOM

165 West 26th St
212 229 1948
www.sidgolds.com
Open Mon–Fri 5pm–2am,
Sat 7pm–2am, Sun 7pm–12am

Sid Gold's Request Room has all the stylish flair of a mid-century piano bar, but don't expect to hear show tunes or jazz standards here. This contemporary take on a vintage concept is the dream of former Psychedelic Furs and Ramones keyboardist Joe McGinty, who can be found playing 'piano karaoke' here from 9pm, four nights a week on a Baldwin baby grand, belting out pop, rock and post-punk favourites, from the Smiths, David Bowie and Elvis Presley to Nine Inch Nails. A spin around the venue's Instagram account reveals an enthusiastic celebrity clientele joining civilians at the mic, so you never know who you'll bump into. Sit around the piano or in a booth, and enjoy cocktails and a basic list of wines with a menu of sweetly nostalgic food, like shrimp cocktails, pigs in blankets, Waldorf salad and chocolate chip cookies.

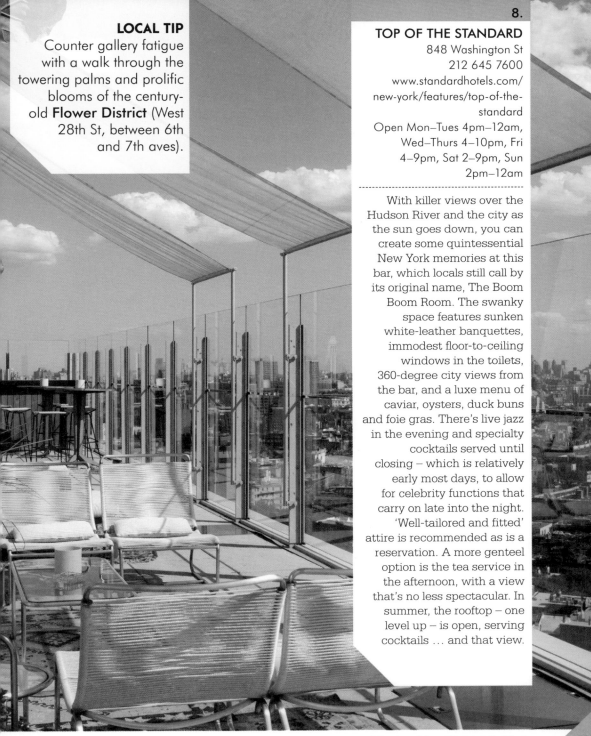

LOCAL TIP

Counter gallery fatigue with a walk through the towering palms and prolific blooms of the century-old **Flower District** (West 28th St, between 6th and 7th aves).

TOP OF THE STANDARD

848 Washington St
212 645 7600
www.standardhotels.com/
new-york/features/top-of-the-
standard
Open Mon–Tues 4pm–12am,
Wed–Thurs 4–10pm, Fri
4–9pm, Sat 2–9pm, Sun
2pm–12am

With killer views over the Hudson River and the city as the sun goes down, you can create some quintessential New York memories at this bar, which locals still call by its original name, The Boom Boom Room. The swanky space features sunken white-leather banquettes, immodest floor-to-ceiling windows in the toilets, 360-degree city views from the bar, and a luxe menu of caviar, oysters, duck buns and foie gras. There's live jazz in the evening and specialty cocktails served until closing – which is relatively early most days, to allow for celebrity functions that carry on late into the night. 'Well-tailored and fitted' attire is recommended as is a reservation. A more genteel option is the tea service in the afternoon, with a view that's no less spectacular. In summer, the rooftop – one level up – is open, serving cocktails … and that view.

One of the city's most stunning public spaces is also its most unusual – **The High Line** is a 2.3 kilometre- (1.43 mile-) long park built on an elevated rail line running 9 metres (29 feet) above the road, from Gansevoort Street in the Meatpacking District to West 34th Street in Chelsea. It has 11 access points along the way – four with elevators. Beautiful year-round, it's particularly lush in spring and summer, when it can become especially crowded on weekends. There are sculptures to enjoy along the way, more than 350 plant species, nine seasonal food vendors, lawns, lounges and transparent viewing platforms to catch the bustling city below.

For the best look at American art of the 20th and 21st centuries, visit the **Whitney Museum** (99 Gansevoort St), housed since 2015 in a striking Renzo Piano–designed building (also famed as the architect of Paris' Pompidou and London's Shard). In addition to holding the world's most comprehensive Edward Hopper collection (more than 3000 works) and works by Georgia O'Keeffe, Jasper Johns and Mark Rothko in its solid permanent collection, the museum is famed for its survey of contemporary art in the U.S. through the Whitney Biennial – held in even-numbered years. The museum stays open late (until 10pm) on Friday and Saturday nights, with pay-what-you-wish entry on Fridays from 7–9.30pm.

The serene **Rubin Museum** (150 West 17th St) is dedicated to the collection, display and preservation of art from the Himalayas and India. Its permanent collection is focused mostly on works from Tibet. Entry is free on Fridays from 6–10pm. The museum's Cafe Serai hosts Himalayan Happy Hour every Wednesday, from 6–9pm, with live music. On Fridays it offers an Asian menu with a martini and wine bar, DJs and gallery tours.

Contemporary dance lovers should check the program at **The Joyce Theater** (175 8th Ave), showcasing emerging and established dancers from around the world.

Circumnavigate the island of Manhattan in a 1920s-style ferry on an **Architect Guild Boat Tour**, while enjoying a glass of champagne and lively narration by members of the American Institute of Architects. Tours depart from Chelsea Piers (Pier 62, at West 22nd St).

If you're not too tired from pounding the pavements, **Chelsea Piers** (23rd St and Hudson River Park) is a six-block complex where you can play beach volleyball, baseball, rock climbing, a golf driving range, ice skating, bowling and yoga.

Wander among more than 200 independent art galleries, with most found between 10th and 11th Avenues, from West 20th to West 28th Streets, where you can enjoy museum-quality work in more intimate settings.

Map Labels

CHELSEA

23RD STREET C E

The GEM Hotel

WEST
WEST
WEST

8TH AVENUE

20TH STREET
21ST STREET

19TH STREET

Linda Gross Theater

LinkNYC

THE JOYCE THEATER

18TH STREET

LinkNYC

Maritime Hotel

WEST

17TH STREET

LinkNYC

Doctor Gertrude B Kelly Playground

LinkNYC

16TH STREET

15TH STREET

LinkNYC

14TH STREET– 8TH AVENUE A C E L

LinkNYC

Jackson Square Park

14TH STREET

1 2 3

14TH STREET

7TH AVENUE

WEST

Main Text

This vibrant precinct boasts stately 19th century Victorian-style homes, renowned landmark parks like Union Square, Gramercy Park and Madison Square Park, prestigious shopping and top-tier dining. The twenty blocks between East 14th and East 34th streets take in Union Square, Gramercy and Flatiron.

From the **Theodore Roosevelt Birthplace Museum** (see p. 106) to the iconic **Flatiron Building** (see p. 106) and famed live rock venues like **Irving Plaza** and **Gramercy Theater** (see p. 106), this area is bursting at the seams with living history and places to be discovered.

14th St; 23rd St

*Different station locations for different subway lines

Listings

SHOP
1 ABC Carpet & Home
2 Strand Book Store

SHOP & EAT
3 Eataly

EAT
4 Shake Shack
5 Gramercy Tavern

EAT & DRINK
6 Chanson

DRINK
7 The Raines Law Room
8 Nomad Bar

UNION SQUARE, GRAMERCY & FLATIRON

1.
ABC CARPET & HOME

888 Broadway
212 473 3000
www.abchome.com
Open Mon–Wed & Fri–Sat
10am–7pm, Thurs 10am–8pm,
Sun 10am–6pm

At ABC Home you can feel good about decorating your home and protecting our planet at the same time. This multi-level department store specialises in contemporary and vintage pieces with an emphasis on artisanship, Indigenous cultures and ethical manufacturing. You may think you've entered a deluxe bazaar overflowing with carefully curated furnishings, jewellery, gifts, clothing and other textiles sourced from around the world. So unique is the retail space, it's often described as resembling a museum or a sanctuary. A mezzanine-level 'Deepak Homebase' also hosts lively salon-style events, under wellness guru Deepak Chopra. The focus on wellbeing extends to the basement, where you can enjoy a meal in one of Michelin-star chef Jean-George Vongerichten's three eateries covering a range budgets: the sophisticated farm-to-table restaurant **ABC Kitchen**; tapas-style **ABC Cocina**, and the new plant-based cafe **abcV**. (www.abchome.com/dine/).

2.
STRAND BOOK STORE

828 Broadway
212 473 1452
www.strandbooks.com
Open Mon–Sat 9.30am–
10.30pm, Sun 11am–10.30pm

If you're the type of person who spends hours in a good bookshop, you may have to notify your next of kin before you cross the threshold of the Strand. This isn't just any bookshop – it's one of *the* bookshops, on par with Shakespeare's in Paris or Foyles or Hatchards in London.

The Strand has been a Broadway institution since 1927, and at this address from 1956. It's slogan is '18 miles of books', and in all reality there are probably more. Search through canyons of tomes and modern coffee table collections.

Particularly noteworthy is its stock of screenplays, graphic novels, design, fashion and photography books on the second floor, but don't forget to explore the dark depths of its basement where you can easily lose hours browsing.

In the age of e-books, it's refreshing to know that one of New York's original bookstores is going strong.

There's regular signings and Q&As. Check their website in advance.

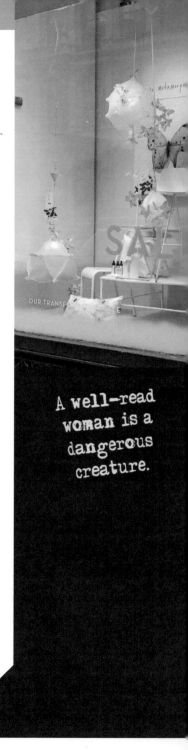

A well-read woman is a dangerous creature.

LOCAL TIP

A visit to **260 Sample** (260 5th Ave) may net you the bargain of the century from one of New York's best designers or big name brands. The range changes weekly, so check their website before you arrive to see if it's a brand you love.

1.

2.

2.

3.

EATALY

200 5th Ave
212 229 2560
www.eataly.com/us_en/stores/
nyc-flatiron
Open Mon–Sun 7am–11pm

An epicurean deli-meets-food court, delivering the freshest Italian produce and cuisine this side of Italia, all curated by a celebrity chef. As one of the trailblazers of the food hall resurgence, it brings together counter after counter of fine Italian flavours, from aged cheeses to freshly butchered, *Flintstones*-sized tomahawk steaks. Weave between barrels stacked tall with Romanesque columns of pungent parmesan wheels or duck below hand-roped provolone hanging from hooks. Taste wafer-thin slices of salamis and cured meats, or visit the fishmonger and choose between razor clams, fresh herb and orange-stuffed bronzino, or select your own lobster from the tank.

As well as shopping, you can dine in at Eataly. Order homemade gnocchi or coal-fired pizzas, compose a charcuterie plate or sample the catch of the day, and sit back to enjoy a glass of Italian wine as you partake in a little people-watching. For dessert, there's a Nutella cafe with devilishly sweet crepes, and you can take a class at Eataly's very own cooking school, La Scuola.

LOCAL TIP

Visit the rooftop bar and restaurant, **Baita**, for fine Italian wines and share plates. It becomes a pop-up ski lodge in winter.

SHAKE SHACK

Madison Square Park,
Madison Ave & East 23rd St
212 889 6600
www.shakeshack.com
Open Mon–Fri
7.30am–10.30pm, Sat–Sun
8.30am–10.30pm

Contrary to its name, Shake Shack has become a phenomenon for its highly addictive burgers – and this Madison Square Park kiosk is the mothership. Unrecognisable from its humble beginnings as a hot dog cart back in 2001, it attracts queues not just here but at most of its many locations. For the traditionalist, the Shack Burger is recommended – a freshly ground Angus beef patty on a potato roll, with optional salad items to maintain your virtue. But vegetarians and meat-eaters alike swoon over the 'Shroom Burger, with just the right amount of crunch and a centre of gooey cheese.

Besides the burgers, its shakes and 'concretes' (frozen custard blended with 'mix-ins', like fudge sauce, or chocolate truffle cookie dough) are notorious, and even four-legged friends are catered for with the Woof! menu.

5.

GRAMERCY TAVERN

42 East 20th St
212 477 0777
www.gramercytavern.com
Open Sun–Thurs 11.30–11pm,
Fri–Sat 11.30–12am

To sample the best of New York's locally grown produce, look no further. With a Michelin star under the venue's belt, the menus here are seasonal and highlight the best of what's on offer from regional purveyors. It offers two dining concepts – fine dining or a more casual tavern.

The tavern has a welcoming wine bar feel with dark wood accents and stunning floral arrangements. It offers an a la carte menu and the local favourite is the Gramercy Tavern burger, with thick ground beef, layered with rich, melted cheddar cheese and bacon, and the peach cobbler for dessert.

The formal dining room is a quiet, dimly lit space, with dark wood fixtures, large hanging candelabras and arched architraves. There's a fixed price or tasting menu, including smoked trout with kohlrabi and roe, and lamb loin with sunchokes, harissa and ravioli.

If you can't secure a booking in the dining room (at least 28 days' notice), the tavern is walk-in only and doesn't require a wardrobe change.

6.

CHANSON

20 West 23rd St
919 423 8880
www.patisseriechanson.com
Open Mon–Fri 8am–9pm, Sat
9am–8pm, Sun 10am–6pm

Chanson is an ultra-discreet bar, offering the ultimate in nocturnal decadence, with a dessert degustation menu created as you watch and perfectly matched cocktails.

The hidden treasure, which operates at night below a gourmet patisserie, is just starting to be discovered by even the most ardent foodies.

The intimate 16-seat space allows Chanson owner and executive chef, Rory Macdonald, to assemble six mains (plus several amuses bouches) – which progress from savoury to sweet – right in front of guests over the course of a two-hour sitting.

From the burst of gin and tonic served in a rolled-up slice of cucumber, to peanut butter and jelly desserts delivered in a vintage peanut butter jar, all aided by the showmanship of smoke, fire and foams, you'll be as fascinated as you will be fulfilled.

5.

5.

6.

6.

5.

6.

7.

THE RAINES LAW ROOM
48 West 17th St
www.raineslawroom.com
Open Mon–Thurs 5pm–2am,
Fri–Sat 5pm–3am, Sun
7pm–1am

Raines Law Room is the kind of bar you could walk past daily and never know it was there. One of a series of popular New York speakeasies, it captures the romance of prohibition era sly-grog clubs, with its pressed metal ceilings, plush armchairs and tasteful Georgian-era accents.

For added privacy take a chiffon curtained booth and when you're ready to order, pull a lamp string and a waiter will be at your beck and call. The focus is cocktails and the menu is extensive, ordered by region and flavour. Try the 10 Gallon Hat (mescal, pineapple, ancho chili syrup and lime) for deliciously contrasting flavours of smoky bacon and sweet tropical pineapple juice.

Entry is via an unmarked basement doorway with a doorbell to gain access. If there's room, you're ushered in, but if not, you can leave your number to be contacted when your table is ready. You can make reservations for Sunday, Monday and Tuesday only.

NOMAD BAR

10 West 28th St
212 796 1500
www.thenomadhotel.com/
new-york/dining/spaces/
the-nomad-bar
Open Mon–Tues 12pm–12am,
Wed–Fri 12pm–2am, Sat
5pm–12.30am, Sun 5pm–12am

For a decadent Gatsby-like experience, a nod to old money and old school New York with its gold ambient lighting, gold stools, golden olive booths and dark wooden bars, this is the perfect place to rub shoulders with the city's young elite.

While there's no dress code, you certainly want to look the part, especially when you ascend the grand wrought-iron molded staircase to the upper-floor balcony seating for the best views in the house.

The bar offers a selection of finely crafted cocktails created by award-winning mixologist Leo Robitschek, and sports both a voluminous selection of light and dark spirit options, many with a tiki bar look and taste. But it's the large-format cocktails that have the crowds flapping – serving 6–8 people these aptly named 'Cocktail Explosions' are bursting with flavour and made for sharing (including the cost) – but that's what makes a night out so memorable.

WHILE YOU'RE HERE

New York has it all. Explore the history of sexuality or jump for joy on a bouncy house made of rubber breasts at the **Museum of Sex** (233 5th Ave).

President Theodore Roosevelt was the first president to be born in New York City, and he was raised in an apartment in the neighbourhood that was demolished at the turn of the century. In its place is an early 20th-century townhouse that now houses the **Theodore Roosevelt Birthplace Museum** (28 East 20th St) in his honour.

View the **Metronome at Union Square**, a public art piece (and time piece) by Kristin Jones and Andrew Ginzel. It is viewable above the building that houses Best Buy.

Further north in the precinct you'll find one of the world's first skyscrapers, the iconic **Flatiron Building** (175 5th Ave). This sandstone building shaped like an old flat iron is still as elegant today as it was in 1902. And to get a view of the other Big Apple icon, the Empire State Building, head on up to the rooftop bar **230 Fifth** (230 5th Ave). Not only does the outside bar have views to boot, but the cocktails are on point.

If you like your music live and loud, catch a gig at **Gramercy Theater** (127 East 23rd St) or

Irving Plaza (17 Irving Plaza). Both venues host top calibre local and international acts, and more recently reunited nineties to noughties faves. These intimate spaces are the perfect setting to see world-class bands in a local venue.

Union Square Park is normally bustling with activity. The park has a long history of being a centre of political activism, and you'll find statues of political leaders like George Washington and Abraham Lincoln towering over the crowds.

Union Square Greenmarket on 14th Street (between University Place and Park Ave South) runs four days per week (Monday, Wednesday, Friday and Saturday), offering the region's best seasonal produce and is a favourite local market. Stalls offer honey grown on city rooftops, freshly made jams and artisanal whiskeys.

When you think of the Big Apple, it's the hustle and bustle of Midtown Manhattan that comes to mind. The stretch between 34th Street to the south and 59th Street to the north includes many of NYC's biggest drawcards – from the classic department store **Macy's** to **Times Square** (see p. 118), the **Theater District**, **Grand Central Station** (see p. 119), **MoMA** (see p. 118), the **New York Public Library** (see p. 119), **Radio City Music Hall** (see p. 118) and the **Empire State Building**.

Prepare yourself for the delightful chaos of crowds, congestion and food trucks (see p. 114).

Grand Central; 47th–50th Sts–Rockefeller Center; 5th Ave–53rd St
*Different station locations for different subway lines

MAP (left)

West 49th Street
West 48th Street
Ramon Aponte Park
West 47th Street
MIDTOWN
West 46th Street
JOE ALLEN
West 45th Street
West 44th Street
LinkNYC
Row NYC Hotel
Imperial Theatre
West 43rd Street
Hayes Theater
42ND STREET–PORT AUTHORITY BUS TERMINAL Ⓐ Ⓒ Ⓔ
9TH AVENUE
8TH AVENUE

TO MAP RIGHT (VIA WEST 46TH STREET)

MIDTOWN

24   JUN 50T6

SHOP
1 MOMA Design Store
2 Anthropologie
3 Hammacher Schlemmer
4 5th Ave

EAT
5 Joe Allen
6 Food Trucks

EAT & DRINK
7 Grand Central Oyster Bar
DRINK
8 Bar SixtyFive

N

LOUIS VUITTON
TIFFANY & CO.
'Love' sculpture
ABERCROMBIE & FITCH
GUCCI
NIKETOWN NEW YORK
HENRI BENDEL
WEST 55TH
WEST 54TH STREET
MOMA (MUSEUM OF MODERN ART)
The St. Regis New York
LinkNYC
53RD STREET
CBS Building
LinkNYC
LinkNYC
MOMA DESIGN STORE
5TH AVENUE-53RD STREET
E M
RADIO CITY MUSIC HALL
LinkNYC
53RD
Omni Berkshire Place
STREET
BAR SIXTYFIVE
TOP OF THE ROCK
ANTHROPOLOGIE
52ND
47TH-50TH STREETS-ROCKEFELLER CENTER
B D F M
NBC STUDIOS
THE LEGO STORE
EAST 51ST
LinkNYC
MADISON
Prometheus
St Patrick's Cathedral
PARK
WEST 49TH ST
LinkNYC
Saks Fifth Avenue
50TH STREET
TO HAMMACHER SCHLEMMER (NOT SHOWN ON MAP)
WEST 48TH
LinkNYC
AMERICAN GIRL
EAST 49TH STREET
LinkNYC
51ST STREET
6
WEST 47TH STREET
WEST 46TH
MIDTOWN
LinkNYC
MIDTOWN EAST
TO JOE ALLEN (SEE MAP LEFT)
EAST
W Hotel
AVENUE
48TH
Marriott Eastside
0   100 m
MANHATTAN
AVENUE
LinkNYC
5TH
EAST
46TH
47TH
Roger Smith Hotel
LinkNYC
EAST 44TH
45TH
The Roosevelt Hotel
PARK
EAST 43RD STREET
MADISON
GRAND CENTRAL TERMINAL
LEXINGTON
LinkNYC
Fitzpatrick Grand Central Hotel
LinkNYC
Andaz 5th Avenue
42ND
CAMPBELL APARTMENT
LinkNYC
MURRAY HILL
GRAND CENTRAL OYSTER BAR
3RD
STREET
GRAND CENTRAL-42ND STREET
S 4 5 6 7

1.

MOMA DESIGN STORE

44 West 53rd St
212 767 1050
store.moma.org
Open Sun–Thu 9.30am–
6.30pm, Fri–Sat 9.30am–9pm

For lovers of art, design and fashion, a visit to MoMA (the Museum of Modern Art *see* p. 118) is a must and be sure to cross the road to the design store. It's housed in a sparse, minimalist space and is a treasure trove of design books, avant-garde accessories, home furnishings, toys and novelties. With a clear focus on the innovative and interesting, you'll find new technologies like programmable circuit boards for budding IT minds, synths and amplifiers and even digital candlesticks. The kids' section is fascinating and fun for adults too, with toys that inspire creative play and leave you secretly jealous they weren't around a few decades earlier. And for more original souvenirs, there are the museum's prints, shirts and umbrellas featuring some of MoMA's finest pieces by Dali, Warhol, Van Gogh and Lichtenstein.

2.

ANTHROPOLOGIE

50 Rockefeller Plaza
212 246 0386
www.anthropologie.com
Open Mon–Sun 10am–9pm

Anthropologie is an American brand with a global outlook, selling fashion and homewares with a unique, handcrafted feel. Their vast, bi-level flagship store, filled with provincial decor and whimsical women's clothing will soon have you imagining a more free-spirited lifestyle. The bohemian brand offers a great range of separates as well as dresses, which celebrate colour and interesting textiles, and are also available in petite sizing. Vintage-inspired decor is displayed throughout the store in everything from monogrammed cheese boards and decorative ceramics, to cutglass doorknobs and patchwork bedding, evocative of French farms and whitewashed seaside cottages. With some of the stunning pieces commanding a high price, it's a good thing there's a large sales section in the basement, to keep the budget in check.

2.

ANTHROPOLOGIE

1.

1.

3.

HAMMACHER SCHLEMMER

147 East 57th St
212 421 9001
www.hammacher.com
Open Mon–Sat 10am–7pm,
Sun 11am–6pm

New York's the kind of place you can buy almost anything, and this is the store where you'll find the completely unimaginable.

Since 1848 Hammacher Schlemmer has been sourcing the weird, wonderful and the rare for well-heeled New Yorkers. Originally a mail-order catalogue company specialising in tools, their shop is an Aladdin's cave of treasures. Hanging from the walls are hovercraft golf buggies, an orca submarine and ride-on iceboxes. A Zoltar fortune telling machine (like in the movie, *Big*) offers to tell your destiny, or splurge on a New York hotdog cart, a carousel or possibly a carnival calliope, and there's even a flying bicycle.

And while some items, like the genuine London black cab or the inflatable Irish pub, come with big price tags, there are plenty of affordable knick-knacks, collectibles and even handy travel tools. You can buy water-powered dental flossers and the latest electric toothbrush – this is the place that introduced New Yorkers to the pop-up toaster.

4.

5TH AVE

Manhattan's famed 5th Avenue is acclaimed globally as a shopper's paradise. Window shop the flagship stores of internationally renowned fashion brands like **Tiffany and Co** (no. 727), **Gucci** (no. 725), **Louis Vuitton** (corner of E57th St) and **Abercrombie & Fitch** (no.720), alongside historic department stores like Saks (no.611), **Henri Bendel** (no.712) and **Bergdorf Goodman** (no.754).

At the **Lego** flagship store (no. 620), a Lego Rockefeller Plaza is watched over by hero of Gotham, Lego Batman. Young (and old) imaginations will be sparked by the vast 'Pick a Brick' wall, and the large format models from *The Simpsons*, *Star Wars* and *Harry Potter*.

At American Girl (just off 5th Ave at 75 Rockefeller Plaza), each doll has her own unique story, wardrobe and accessories that reflect an aspect of American history, with the company, in recent years, creating characters that reflect women and girl's empowerment. Book ahead for the popular salon experience, where children and their dolls can be given matching makeovers, hairstyles and ear piercings.

5.

JOE ALLEN

326 West 46th St
212 581 6464
www.joeallenrestaurant.com
Open Mon–Tues 12–4pm,
Wed 11.30am–4pm,
Thurs–Fri 12–4pm, Sat–Sun
11.30am–4pm (lunch);
Sun–Thurs 4–11.45pm & Fri–Sat
4pm–12am (dinner)

Joe Allen, established in 1965, is the resident stalwart, delivering on service, price, and schedule for a traditional pre- or post-theatre meal.

The restaurant celebrates the glory days of old Broadway but ironically, the walls are adorned with framed prints of Broadway flops. Below them exposed brick melds into worn wooden flooring and white tablecloths. Broadway casts and crews can be spotted among the restaurant's regulars and another claim to fame is that celebrity chef Bobby Flay got his start here.

While its burgers are a menu staple, those in the know order the meatloaf – don't worry, it's a far cry from the dry, over-baked loaves you've repressed from your childhood. This signature dish is well seasoned and served alongside a mound of silky mashed potatoes.

Reservations are hard to get, particularly near showtimes. Be sure to book up to seven days in advance.

FOOD TRUCKS

Vendors of New York's famed street food (known locally as 'street meat') now offer so much more than day-old hot dogs and soggy knishes. These mobile food courts bring together flavours from around the world and can be found close to major attractions like Bryant Park, around 34th St, and at the 59th St entrances to Central Park. Most also advertise their locations via Twitter and Instagram.

Some local faves include the traditional gyros from the **Halal Guys** (West 53rd St and 6th Ave and other locations across Manhattan via thehalalguys.com/locations/), **Korilla BBQ** (@KorillaBBQ) with their Korean-Mexican fusion Bulgogi burritos, and dessert favourite, **Wafels & Dinges**, dishing up hot waffles dripping with indulgent toppings like Belgian chocolate fudge. There are queues (not uncommon in Midtown) but if there is a line-up, it's almost a guarantee that the food will be worth the wait. The offerings are ever-expanding and the range of trucks differ daily, so browse their menus, pick up a bite and find a quiet place local to it, like Bryant Park or Central Park, to dine.

7.

GRAND CENTRAL OYSTER BAR

89 East 42nd St
212 490 6650
www.oysterbarny.com
Open Mon–Sat 11.30am–
9.30pm

Lauded as much for its classic design and heritage as it is for its fresh primo shellfish, the Grand Central Oyster Bar dates back to 1913, opening three weeks after Grand Central Terminal's ribbon cutting ceremony. Right up to the 1960s, it was the place to eat before or after a long-haul train ride. Today its vaulted ceiling with interlocking tile work has been renovated to its former glory; the menu is printed daily and the boards change as new catches come in.

Sit in the restaurant, at one of the bars or at the U-shaped shucking stations, where your 'captain' will serve you up freshly shucked oysters, clams and mussels. Try between 20 and 50 unique molluscs and shellfish from Maine to Chesapeake Bay. While the Manhattan Clam Chowder makes for a warming starter, be sure to try the melt-in-your-mouth sea scallops in garlic butter or the shrimp cocktail. For the full *Mad Men* experience, check out the saloon with its dated yet timeless decor, model ships and fishing ephemera.

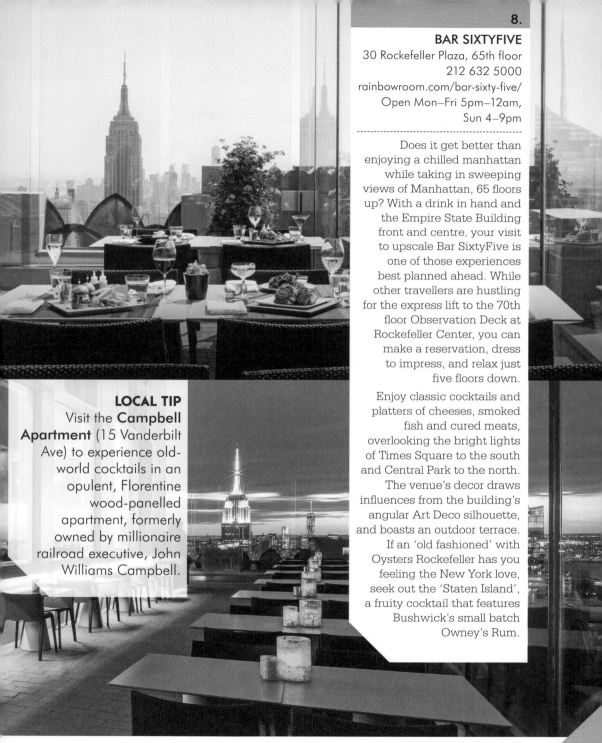

BAR SIXTYFIVE
30 Rockefeller Plaza, 65th floor
212 632 5000
rainbowroom.com/bar-sixty-five/
Open Mon–Fri 5pm–12am,
Sun 4–9pm

Does it get better than enjoying a chilled manhattan while taking in sweeping views of Manhattan, 65 floors up? With a drink in hand and the Empire State Building front and centre, your visit to upscale Bar SixtyFive is one of those experiences best planned ahead. While other travellers are hustling for the express lift to the 70th floor Observation Deck at Rockefeller Center, you can make a reservation, dress to impress, and relax just five floors down.

Enjoy classic cocktails and platters of cheeses, smoked fish and cured meats, overlooking the bright lights of Times Square to the south and Central Park to the north.
The venue's decor draws influences from the building's angular Art Deco silhouette, and boasts an outdoor terrace.
If an 'old fashioned' with Oysters Rockefeller has you feeling the New York love, seek out the 'Staten Island', a fruity cocktail that features Bushwick's small batch Owney's Rum.

LOCAL TIP
Visit the **Campbell Apartment** (15 Vanderbilt Ave) to experience old-world cocktails in an opulent, Florentine wood-panelled apartment, formerly owned by millionaire railroad executive, John Williams Campbell.

You'll be amazed at how many famous works are housed under one roof at the **Museum of Modern Art (MoMA)** (11 West 53rd St), including Van Gogh's *Starry Night* and Dali's *Persistence of Memory*. MoMA is open daily between 10.30am and 5.30pm, and until 8pm on Friday when it's free from 4pm year-round, but be prepared to queue.

An unassuming subway grate on the southwest corner of Lexington Avenue and 52nd street is where Marilyn Monroe's white halter dress was blown over her hips by the passing 6 train below in *Seven Year Itch*. For other classic movie sites, drop past **Tiffany's** (727 5th Ave) for breakfast (yes, they actually serve breakfast there now) and the **Plaza Hotel** (768 5th Ave), where a young Macaulay Culkin bumped into a future President Trump in *Home Alone 2*.

Times Square (42nd–47th St, intersection of Broadway and 7th Ave) can be seen from space and is watched over by a real-time Earth Camera so you can give your family and friends back home a cheeky wave. For discount Broadway tickets, queue at the **TKTS booth** (or try the one downtown at South Street Seaport where you can get the same great prices without the lines).

Visit the **Top of the Rock** (30 Rockefeller Plaza) observation deck for sweeping panoramic views of Manhattan, Central Park and the iconic Empire State Building. While you are here, take a tour of the **NBC Studios** downstairs or plan ahead and book a place in the audience of one of the *Tonight Show* tapings.

Radio City Music Hall (1260 6th Ave) is where the *Ed Sullivan Show* and many classic live performances were broadcast across America. It is now a designated New York landmark and cultural treasure. Take a tour to experience its opulent Art Deco interior.

The **Garment District** (the streets between West 35th St and 42nd St, bordered by 7th and 9th Avenues) is still the go-to for fashion designers and hobbyists looking for particular fabrics or accessories – there's even a place called Spandex World. The **Flower District** (West 28th St between Avenue of the Americas and 7th Ave) is home to an urban jungle of lush horticultural specialists and florists, while the **Diamond District** (47th St between 5th Ave and Avenue of the Americas) is a block of jewellers and diamond cutters.

Grand Central Station is an architectural treasure dating back to the golden age of rail travel. Marvel at the great Celestial Ceiling, test out the acoustics in the Whispering Gallery or check out the fresh markets and food court.

The New York Public Library (476 5th Ave), guarded by two marble lions, is primarily a research library but the public is allowed to quietly walk the stacks and reading rooms immortalised in numerous films, including the original *Ghostbusters*.

Bryant Park, just behind the library, makes a great rest stop, with free movies in the summer, occasional live performances and a winter village with ice-skating rink and seasonal treats over the Christmas period.

Hudson
River

Riverside
Park

NYC
Parks

WEST 79TH

ZABARS

LinkNYC

79TH
STREET

HAMMER
BOY

Hotel
Belleclaire

WEST 75TH

NYLO
Hotel

WEST 74TH

LinkNYC

Riverside
Park
South

WEST 73RD

BEACON
THEATRE

72ND
STREET

UPPER
WEST
SIDE

LinkNYC

THE DAKOTA
APARTMENTS

Merkin
Concert
Hall

72ND STREET

MAGNOLIA
BAKERY

WEST 66TH ST

WEST 69TH STREET

LinkNYC

LinkNYC

66TH STREET-
LINCOLN
CENTER

American
Folk Art
Museum

86TH
STREET

UPPER
EAST SIDE

The Upper East Side has traditionally bee
home to New York's socialites, old money
and the highest quotient of designer
handbags and fluffy lap dogs per capita.

Between 5th Avenue and Park Avenue, you'll find
the **Metropolitan Museum of Art** (see p. 130)
and the **Guggenheim** (see p. 131), which are
reason enough for most travellers to visit. Explore
the famed shopping avenues of Park Avenue and
Lexington Avenue, with their luxe boutiques and fin
dining restaurants, or wander leafy side streets line
with foreign embassies, stately brownstones and the
offices of plastic surgeons. The Upper East Side als
offers plenty of cosmopolitan dining options and
inviting local bars.

 59th St–Lexington Ave; 77th St; 86th St

*Different station locations for different subway lines

24   JUN 8016

SHOP
1 KITCHEN ARTS AND LETTERS
2 TENDER BUTTONS
EAT
3 CAFÉ SABARSKY
4 CANDLE CAFE
5 BLUESTONE LANE

DRINK
6 HEIDI'S HOUSE BY THE SIDE
OF THE ROAD
7 BEMELMANS BAR
8 BRANDY'S PIANO BAR

UPPER
WEST
SIDE

86TH
STREET
Ⓑ Ⓒ 🚇

West Avenue

Columbus

Central Park

81ST STREET-
MUSEUM OF
NATURAL
HISTORY
Ⓑ Ⓒ 🚇

The Great Lawn

AMERICAN MUSEUM OF
NATURAL HISTORY

Shakespeare Garden

Turtle Pond

NEW YORK
HISTORICAL
SOCIETY

BELVEDERE
CASTLE

The Lake

Azalea Pond

Cedar Hill

Jacqueline Kennedy Onassis
Reservoir

THE JEWISH
MUSEUM

5TH Avenue

KITCHEN
ARTS AND
LETTERS ⚪

BLUESTONE
LANE 📍

SOLOMON R
GUGGENHEIM
MUSEUM

96TH
STREET
6 🚇

92ND
STREET Y

LinkNYC

Ruppert Park

East 86TH Street

Madison Avenue

86TH
STREET
4 5 6 🚇

LinkNYC

86TH
STREET
📍 Q

CAFÉ
SABARSKY 📍

METROPOLITAN
MUSEUM OF ART

UPPER
EAST
SIDE

Park Avenue

BRANDY'S
PIANO BAR

LinkNYC

3RD Avenue

79TH Street

Bethesda Fountain

Pilgrim Hill

Frisbee Hill

NYC Parks

East 72ND Street

NYC Parks

East Green

The Dene

NYC Parks

CENTRAL
PARK ZOO

Gapston Bridge

Grand Army Plaza

East 59TH St

St Regis
New York

BEMELMANS
BAR 📍

THE MET
BREUER

5TH Avenue

East 72ND Street

Park Avenue Tunnel

THE FRICK
COLLECTION

Madison Avenue

LinkNYC

LinkNYC

Lexington Avenue

LinkNYC

68TH STREET-
HUNTER
COLLEGE
🚇 6

Ⓕ Ⓠ LEXINGTON AV-
63RD STREET
🚇

TENDER
BUTTONS ⚪

4 5 6 59TH
Ⓝ Ⓡ Ⓦ STREET-
LEXINGTON
AVENUE

East

East 57TH St

60TH St

65TH Street

77TH
STREET
6 🚇

CANDLE
CAFE

HEIDI'S
HOUSE BY
THE SIDE OF
THE ROAD ⚪

2ND Avenue

72ND
STREET
🚇 Q

LinkNYC

LinkNYC

St Catherine's
Park

LENNOX
HILL

Caspary
Auditorium

1ST Avenue

York Avenue

FDR Drive

East River

ROOSEVELT
ISLAND

The Bentley
Hotel

East Meadow

0 ———— 250 m

N ↗

121

1.

KITCHEN ARTS AND LETTERS

1435 Lexington Ave
212 876 5550
www.kitchenartsandletters.com
Open Mon 1–6pm, Tues–Fri
10am–6.30pm, Sat 11am–6pm

Ever wondered where New York's greatest chefs spend their free time? Kitchen Arts and Letters was established in 1983 and is a specialist indie bookstore that embraces all there is to love about cookbooks and the culinary arts. On arrival, you'll be taken aback by the breadth of the collection. Towering shelves from floor to ceiling hold titles from around the world as well as a broad cross-section of scholarly titles. Luckily the team are more than happy to share their knowledge and passion for food and cooking and willingly offer their guidance if there's something in particular you're hoping to find; and they're experts in locating out-of-print and hard to find titles. Frequented by the likes of celebrity chef and author Anthony Bourdain, it attracts the who's who of the international food (and foodie) scene.

2.

TENDER BUTTONS

143 East 62nd St
212 758 7004
www.tenderbuttons-nyc.com
Open Mon–Fri 10am–6.30pm,
Sat 10.30am–5.30pm

Hundreds of years of fashion innovation still hasn't been able to top the utilitarian simplicity of the humble button. This small shopfront marked by a large golden button houses a collection of tens of thousands of buttons from decades past and antique button collections from all over the world. These aren't just your average buttons (though there are plenty of those, too). There are artfully ornate, hand-painted buttons, porcelain treasures and ones cast from old silver and nickel coins. It's like a museum-meets-library-meets-specialised-retailer, and it attracts everyone from hobbyists to New York's fashion and costume designers. Tender Buttons is not just a resource to replace that missing button from your favourite vintage piece – it's about reinventing, redefining and personalising your look. Here you're sure to find buttons that will complete your shirt, blouse or britches.

2.

1.

2.

3.

CAFÉ SABARSKY
(AT NEUE GALERIE)
1048 5th Ave
212 288 0665
www.neuegalerie.org/cafes/
sabarsky
Open Mon 9am–6pm,
Wed 9am–6pm, Thurs–Sun
9am–9pm

- -

This beautiful re-imagination of a Viennese kaffeehaus can be found at a mecca of avant-garde German and Austrian art, the Neue Galerie (*see* p. 131). The cafe is named in honour of one of the museum's founding fathers, art dealer Serge Sabarsky, and is overseen by Austrian chef, Kurt Gutenbrunner.

A Bosendorfer grand piano dominates the cafe entrance and is used for music performances at the Neue Galerie. Inside, the vibe is Viennese parlour, with dark wood-panelled walls, sconce downlighting and cosy booths. On display on a wide marble mantel is an irresistible range of desserts, including linzer torte and strudel. With its prime position looking out across 5th Avenue to Central Park, expect to pay a premium, but it's hard to turn down a steaming hot bowl of goulash soup served with potato pancakes.

LOCAL TIP
If the queues are too long, **Cafe Fledermaus** on the floor below offers an identical menu, though it lacks Sabarsky's ambience.

CANDLE CAFE

1307 3rd Ave
212 472 0970
www.candlecafe.com
Open Mon–Fri 11.30am–
10pm, Sat 9am–10pm, Sun
9am–9.30pm

A favourite with celebrities, reviewers and locals, Candle Cafe offers vegan dishes from ethically-sourced ingredients, and something for every taste and dietary requirement.

Under the entrance's bright purple awning, a golden logo of a leaf, styled to look like the flame of a candle, evokes the restaurant's noble culinary mission. Inside, wholesome treats like porcini mushroom stroganoff or the grilled cheese with a spicy tomato soup (gluten-free) will satisfy your hunger.

On the weekend, start the day right with a healthy brunch like the raw oatmeal with almond milk, chia seeds and fresh berries or the French toast that uses almond cream. They also offer a flight of wellness 'shots' – heavy on the clean and green rather than any alcohol content.

If you love the food, take home their cookbook or visit their other venues on the Upper West Side, and on 79th Street on the Upper East Side.

5.

BLUESTONE LANE
2 East 90th St
646 869 7812
www.bluestonelane.com/cafes/
upper-east-side
Open Mon–Sun 7.30am–6pm

Bluestone Lane has certainly played a big part in popularising smashed avocado on toast and flat whites in NYC. From humble beginnings in the financial district in 2010, it is the brainchild of former Australian Football League (AFL) player Nick Stone, and has grown to more than 10 locations, including this welcome addition to the Museum Mile, housed in a 19th century sandstone church.

It offers affordable all-day, menu items incorporating genuine Australian delicacies and top-rate Melbourne-style coffees. Where else can you get vegemite on toast, lamingtons and warming treats like freshly baked banana bread topped with whipped ricotta, fresh fruit and nuts that could easily win at most country bake-offs. For an extra indulgent treat, try the Aussie iced latte, a cold milk coffee complete with a shot of Bluestone's own grind and topped with a scoop of vanilla ice-cream.

HEIDI'S HOUSE BY THE SIDE OF THE ROAD

308 East 78th St
212 249 0069
www.heidishouse.net
Open Mon 5–10pm, Tues–
Thurs 5–11pm, Fri 5pm–12am,
Sat 4pm–12am, Sun 4–10pm

In a city where living in a shoebox-sized apartment is the norm, Heidi's is a welcome extension of your living space, with gourmet comfort foods and a friendly neighbourhood setting frequented mainly by locals and in-the-know foodies. There are only a few tables and bar seating, which ensures it's always cosy.

Traditional American comfort favourites are elevated, with the must-have mac-and-cheese given an earthy warmth with the addition of porcini mushrooms and truffle oil (and bacon if you're prepared to walk it off the next day).

For dessert, you'll have to toss a coin to choose between the chocolate soufflé and the date pudding – or share and sample off each other's plates.

The wine list is well curated and there's a generous range of beers.

While they don't take formal reservations, you can leave your name and they'll call you when there's a space ready.

7.

BEMELMANS BAR (AT THE CARLYLE HOTEL)

35 East 76th St
212 744 1600
www.rosewoodhotels.com/en/
the-carlyle-new-york/dining/
bemelmans-bar
Open Mon 12pm–12.30am,
Tues–Thurs 12pm–1am,
Fri–Sat 12pm–1.30am, Sun
12pm–12.30am

As you step into the Art Deco Bemelmans Bar, you will be greeted by a white-jacketed attendant and an extensive drinks menu, as the bar's pianist finds just the appropriate jazz for your entrance. It's like a gateway to a bygone era, named after Ludwig Bemelmans, the creator of the children's book series *Madeline*, and a famed *New York Times* illustrator. In 1939 he negotiated 18 months' worth of accommodation here in exchange for painting the bar in his inimitable style, depicting life in New York.

While the dimly lit booths and tables are intimate, a seat at the bar gives you the best view of both Bemelmans' illustrations and the mixologists as they deliver flawless cocktail creations. Arrive early to avoid the cover charge and expect to pay a premium on nights when bands perform, with major players in the jazz scene in residency much of the year.

BRANDY'S PIANO BAR
235 East 84th St
212 744 4949
www.brandyspianobar.com
Open Mon–Sun 4pm–4am

Brandy's is a self-confessed 'good time saloon', a local hang that comes alive every night after nine. It's been a bar for more than a hundred years and a speakeasy during the Prohibition – there are still relics from the time, including the lamps above the bar that have been converted from gas to electricity. It retains an old-world feel with its dark wood panels with deep red painted walls, minimal lighting and Toulouse Lautrec prints.

Instead of the traditional jazz standards and show tunes, Brandy's is about crowd-pleasing classic rock and pop, and it's not uncommon for people to jump up and take over the microphone, karaoke-style. This is what keeps the regulars filing in before the 9.30pm cover and two drink minimum kicks in, and it's what attracts the occasional visit from big name celebrities who love the dark space, flowing cocktails and raucous singalongs as much as the locals.

Central Park is New York's premier green space. With 843 hectares to roam, there's something for everyone here. Lose yourself in the thick scrubby forest of **The Rambles' pathways** where you'll forget the rest of the city exists, rent a boat or watch others row the lake from the comfort of the **Boathouse Restaurant** and climb the ramparts of 19th century ornamental folly, the **Belvedere Castle** for stunning views of the meadows. A jog along the perimeter of the **Jacqueline Kennedy Onassis Reservoir** makes for a memorable workout. Kids will enjoy a visit to the **Central Park Zoo** to watch sea lions and grizzly bears, or a ride on the park's original **Friedsam Carousel** that dates back to 1871.

Fifth Avenue, where it runs adjacent to the east side of Central Park, is known as **Museum Mile**; it's dotted with world-renowned cultural insitutions, that appeal to a variety of art and design lovers.

The Metropolitan Museum of Art (1000 5th Ave) has an elaborate collection of art and artefacts spanning the last 5000 years. Browse themed wings focusing on medieval and Renaissance history through to rooms of Rembrandt, Degas, Van Gogh and Picasso.

The **Met Breuer** (945 Madison Ave), sister site to the Met and only a hop, skip and a jump away on Madison, expands the collection by running the gamut of 20th to 21st century art.

Nearby, you can spend hours gazing at European sculpture and artwork in **The Frick Collection** (1 East 70th St), one of the last 'pay as you wish' museums (Wednesday afternoons only).

Make the pilgrimage to 89th Street and 5th Avenue for the iconic Frank Lloyd Wright designed, **Solomon R. Guggenheim Museum** (1071 5th Ave). Its unique corkscrew ramp design transports you through an extensive collection of modern art dating from Cezanne through to contemporary artists like Marina Abramovic.

The **Jewish Museum** (1109 5th Ave) houses over 30,000 artefacts that examine Jewish heritage and history right back to the Old Testament.

Celebrating culture and the arts in the Big Apple, **92nd Street Y** (1395 Lexington Ave) offers hands-on classes for young and old, and is famed for its 'fireside chats' that allow attendees to get up close and personal with celebrities of the day.

The **Neue Galerie** (1048 5th Ave) is home to the best collection of works from the Viennese school outside of Austria. The gallery includes the golden masterworks of Gustav Klimt and paintings and prints by Oskar Kokoschka, Paul Klee and Vasily Kandinsky. It also includes early 20th century fine and decorative arts from Austrian and German artists dating between the First and Second World Wars.

For a tasty side step away from all that culture, visit the **Sprinkles Cupcakes ATM** (780 Lexington Ave), a teller machine that delivers sweet, creamy cupcakes fresh 24/7 when you swipe your credit card.

WEST
NEW
YORK

ANTHONY M. DEFINO WAY

PORT IMPERIAL BOULEVARD

AVENUE AT PORT IMPERIAL

HUDSON RIVER WATERFRONT WALKWAY

Hudson River

UPPER
WE*T *IDE

The Upper West Side is home to a wealth of culture, spectacular old money architecture and a quieter residential feel. It's where you will find treasures like John Lennon's former residence (*see p. 142*) and the **American Museum of Natural History** (*see p. 143*), which should not be missed.

This precinct is a beacon for the performing arts – it's where you can catch free daily student recitals at the prestigious Juilliard School of Music, experience masterful orchestral and operatic performances at the **Lincoln Center** (*see p. 142*), catch live comedy and rock gigs at the Beacon Theater or chill to the best local talent in a hidden jazz club.

 59th St–Columbus Circle; 66th St–Lincoln Center; 81st St–Museum of Natural History
*Different station locations for different subway lines

24   JUN 8076

*HOP
1 CENTURY 21
*HOP & EAT
2 THE *HOPS AT COLUMBUS CIRCLE

17

EAT
3 LEVAIN BAKERY
4 BARNEY GREENGRASS
5 BAR BOULUD
6 PEACEFOOD CAFE
DRINK
7 MANHATTAN CRICKET CLUB
8 DIZZY'S CLUB COCA-COLA

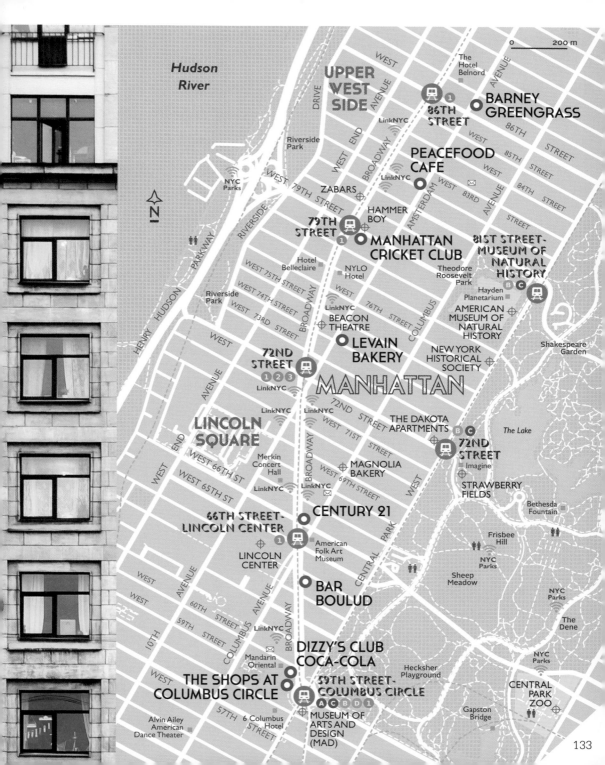

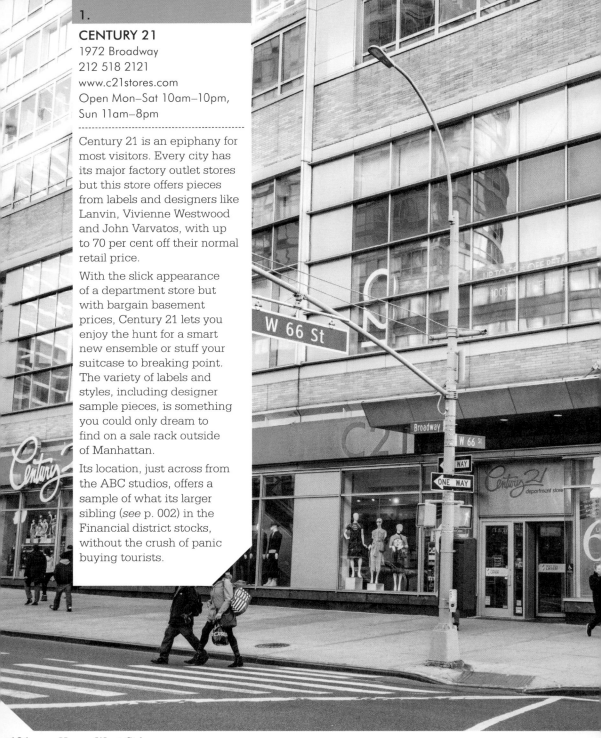

1.

CENTURY 21
1972 Broadway
212 518 2121
www.c21stores.com
Open Mon–Sat 10am–10pm,
Sun 11am–8pm

- -

Century 21 is an epiphany for most visitors. Every city has its major factory outlet stores but this store offers pieces from labels and designers like Lanvin, Vivienne Westwood and John Varvatos, with up to 70 per cent off their normal retail price.

With the slick appearance of a department store but with bargain basement prices, Century 21 lets you enjoy the hunt for a smart new ensemble or stuff your suitcase to breaking point. The variety of labels and styles, including designer sample pieces, is something you could only dream to find on a sale rack outside of Manhattan.

Its location, just across from the ABC studios, offers a sample of what its larger sibling (*see* p. 002) in the Financial district stocks, without the crush of panic buying tourists.

THE SHOPS AT COLUMBUS CIRCLE

Time Warner Center
10 Columbus Circle
212 823 6300
www.theshopsatcolumbus
circle.com
Open Mon–Sat 10am–10pm,
Sun 10am–8pm

At Central Park's south-west corner, this relatively new addition brings together some fine fashion labels, including **Cole Haan**, **Stuart Weitzman** and **Ted Baker** in an up-market galleria accessible via the major transport hub below at 59th Street Columbus Circle station.

After a spot of shopping, stock up for a picnic in Central Park at the well-loved **Whole Foods** market or, for a special treat, make a reservation at Thomas Keller's three-Michelin starred French restaurant, **Per Se**, an experience you'll write home about. It offers a daily lunch or dinner seating for its nine-course tasting menu (or matching vegetable menu for vegetarians). Be sure to wear your best.

For something a little more low-key, try celebrity chef Marc Murphy's **Landmarc** for reasonably priced French-Mediterranean bistro fare. Dress is smart casual and reservations can often be snagged with a few days' notice.

3.

LEVAIN BAKERY

164 West 74th St
212 874 6080
www.levainbakery.com
Open Mon–Sat 8am–7pm,
Sun 9am–7pm

One of the most polarising questions for cookie aficionados is, what makes the perfect cookie? Crunchy? Gooey? Or overloaded with chocolate? Levain has nailed it all in one cookie.

This tiny standing room only bakery is a magnet for locals seeking the perfect cookie and coffee. Best known for the chocolate chip walnut cookie, the bakers here have perfected these sweet treats. Bite into the large mound of soft and semi-baked gooey dough with a surprisingly crunchy cooked shell to reveal a melted blend of choc chunks and chopped walnuts.

Other pastries are also on offer, including crepe pizzas, drizzled in the most decadent of toppings, but not so travel-friendly if you're on the go.

BARNEY GREENGRASS

541 Amsterdam Ave
212 724 4707
www.barneygreengrass.com
Open Tues–Sun 8am–6pm

With the Upper West Side being home to a large Jewish community, you know you're getting the real deal when you buy your lox, bagels and blintzes from a deli that has been serving up New York's best smoked fish since 1909. Barney Greengrass has a familiar, lived-in ambience, coupled with old sacks and crates that give the feeling that nothing has changed in more than 100 years. That familiarity could also come from its starring role as a popular setting for films and TV shows including *Law and Order Criminal Intent* and *30 Rock*. The cramped interior is divided into a separate dining room, the old butter and dairy bar, with etched glass cabinets and cluster of homey 1960s-era kitchen tables and chairs, and a cold bar serving up traditional poppy seed and everything bagels along with the deli's famous platters of smoked lox, sturgeon and white fish.

Proprietor Moe Greengrass handles the till, exchanging good humoured banter with his regulars. It's casual, it's crowded and the bagels and blintzes are well worth the subway ride.

LOCAL TIP

Sweet tooths should head to **Magnolia Bakery** (Columbus Ave at 69th St) to indulge in their famous banana puddings. You can get mini portions to go if you're worried about time or your waistline.

5.

BAR BOULUD

1900 Broadway
212 595 0303
www.barboulud.com/nyc
Open Mon–Fri 11.30–12am,
Sat 11–12am, Sun 11am–10pm

Step inside this French bistro of celebrity chef Daniel Boulud, and you'll feel like you're inside a modern 21st century wine cave, with its dome-shaped roof and saturated warm yellow and burnt orange hues, reminiscent of the French Basque region.

The menu is traditional French fare with a modern flair. A fan favourite is the beef bourguignon, with pearl onions, tender root vegetables and melt-in-your-mouth beef, slow-cooked and coated in a rich, velvety sauce and, in my humble opinion, best served with a side of mash. It's easy to overindulge when you have to choose from traditional favourites like duck à l'orange and the creamy moules au poulette that are bursting with flavour. If you're brave, try to find enough room to squeeze in the baked alaska before waving your white napkin in defeat.

6.

PEACEFOOD CAFE

460 Amsterdam Ave
212 362 2266
www.peacefoodcafe.com
Open Mon–Sun 10am–10pm

This local vegan restaurant dishes up gluten-free and wholesome slow-food meals, and caters to vegans and vegetarians with tasty plant-based treats. Light, airy decor, books, prints and local artwork create the perfect hidey-hole that buffers you from the intensity of Amsterdam Avenue.

The menu is warm and fresh, and the friendly staff, all exude a positive vibe befitting the cafe name. Try the chickpea fries served with ranch sauce, vegan pastries and gluten free dumplings.

When the mercury drops, the red bean chilli is the perfect way to defrost and reset after braving the icy breezes that come right off the Hudson River.

LOCAL TIP
For high tastes on a low budget, opt for **Epicerie Boulud** (Lincoln Center, 1900 Broadway) for a mouthwatering, French-inspired breakfast or lunch, along with chef Daniel Boulud's signature sweet treats. Or you can take-out.

5.

6.

6.

7.

MANHATTAN CRICKET CLUB

226 West 79th St
646 823 9252
www.mccnewyork.com
Open Mon–Sat 6pm–2am

In a city obsessed with baseball, a prestigious cricket club is an unlikely bedfellow, let alone one that attracts card-carrying members. Thousands of expat Australians live in Manhattan and they've brought some of their favourite flavours.

Inside, the decor is elegantly old school, like a 19th century terrace house. Platters of oysters and small plates like the roasted bone marrow are the order of the day. Wash that down with wines from Australia and New Zealand, or sample the bountiful cocktail menu with cheeky names like Bend My Elbow (Strawberry and hibiscus infused no.3 gin, lime, grapefruit bitters and club soda). An unexpected touch is the row of private liquor lockers where members can store their favourite booze.

Reservations are only available for members, but if you're lucky, you may score a table as a walk-in. There are rules and etiquette to adhere to, so dress appropriately, behave nicely and enjoy a night out with a touch of class.

LOCAL TIP
The club is hidden above Australian watering hole **Burke and Wills** where you can down ice-cold Australian beers Coopers Sparkling Ale and James Boag's Premium Lager.

DIZZY'S CLUB COCA-COLA

Jazz at Lincoln Center's
Frederick P. Rose Hall
Broadway at 60th St, 5th Floor
212 258 9595
www.jazz.org/dizzys
Open Mon–Sun 7.30pm–late
(set times 7.30pm & 9.30pm,
late sessions Tues–Sat 11.30pm)

If you're after quality jazz in a sophisticated setting, with the New York skyline in the background, then welcome to Dizzy's! Since 1987, the Lincoln Centre has hosted a mix of established, emerging and student jazz musicians.

Upon entry, you'll be shown to a table with a food and drinks menu (note the $10 minimum spend per person). The lights will dim, the floor-to-ceiling windows behind the stage reveal NYC's twinkling lights, and you can sit back to enjoy the talented musicians right in front of you.

Tickets are best booked in advance via their website, and are $20–$45. But the best part of Dizzy's is definitely the late-night sessions, which only demand a $5–$10 cover charge and no advanced bookings. This is when you'll see musicians really let loose, perhaps even try out tracks they're about to record in the studio.

Be sure to catch a classical concert at the **Lincoln Center** (10 Lincoln Center Plaza), home to **The New York Philharmonic** and **Metropolitan Opera**. If you find yourself a little further uptown, you may also be lucky enough to catch an intimate set by contemporary bands and solo artists or even renowned comics, such as Seinfeld, at the lush, ornate vaudeville-era **Beacon Theatre** (2124 Broadway).

With an emphasis on 'making', **The Museum of Art and Design** (2 Columbus Circle) offers myriad interactive exhibits and a collection that spans art, design and craft. Regular studio sessions and hands-on classes with current artists in residence are offered to people with all levels of experience and backgrounds. Admission is charged for those 18 and over, but you can pay as you wish on Thursday evenings.

Central Park West is one of Manhattan's premiere addresses with classic mansions and town houses overlooking the city's green oasis. At 1 West 72nd Street, you'll find **The Dakota Apartments**, home to celebrities and millionaires. It's where John Lennon lived and was tragically assassinated in 1980, and security is still tight. Directly across the road, just inside Central Park, you'll find a fitting memorial, **Strawberry Fields**.

Visit the **New York Historical Society** (170 Central Park West) for its expansive collection celebrating local history, art and culture or its widely popular public programs. It's dwarfed by its neighbour, the **American Museum of Natural History** (Central Park West and 79th St). Explore galleries of gigantic dinosaur skeletons and biological and geological wonders from around the globe, including golden Inca treasures, or lie back and explore the solar system in the impressive **Hayden Planetarium**.

At the upper tip of Manhattan, you'll find **The Met Cloisters** (99 Margaret Corbin Dve), home to much of the Metropolitan Museum of Art's (see p. 130) medieval collection, bringing together three French and Spanish cloisters transported and rebuilt in **Fort Tryon Park**. Though well off the tourist track, this site is worth the trek.

Zabars (2245 Broadway) is on many foodies' lists in its own right, but if you're in the area, check out the store's 79th Street wall to see *Hammer Boy*, the last remaining piece created by renowned street artist Banksy during his 2013 'Better Out Than In' New York City residency.

This upper Manhattan neighbourhood has been the beating heart for African American–led movements – Civil Rights, music, dance, art and literature – since the Harlem Renaissance of the 1920s.

Billie Holiday got her professional break in Harlem, and Malcolm X lived and died here. The vibrant culture still flourishes, particularly on 125th Street around the iconic **Apollo Theater** (see p. 154). In recent decades, people from French-speaking West African countries have migrated here, including a particularly vibrant Senegalese community in the blocks around West 116th Street. Harlem is great to visit for its jazz clubs, soul food, gospel music, brunches, expressive street style and murals.

116th St; 125th St

*Different station locations for different subway lines

110TH STREET
6
TO MAP RIGHT
(VIA TITO PUENTE WAY & CENTRAL PARK NORTH)

TASTINGS SOCIAL PRESENTS MOUNTAIN BIRD

LinkNYC

Poor Richard's Playground

HARLEM

24   JUN 2016

SHOP
1 Flamekeepers Hat Club
2 Malcolm Shabazz Harlem Market
3 Harlem Haberdashery

EAT
4 Sylvia's
5 Tastings Social Presents Mountain Bird
6 Harlem Shake
7 Sugar Hill Creamery
EAT & DRINK
8 Ginny's Supper Club

125TH STREET
A C B D

WEST 126TH STREET
WEST 127TH STREET

LinkNYC

APOLLO THEATER

DR MARTIN LUTHUR KING JR. BOULEVARD

WEST 125TH STREET
LinkNYC
WEST 124TH STREET
WEST 123RD STREET

LinkNYC

THE STUDIO MUSEUM IN HARLEM

SYLVIA'S

MANHATTAN AVENUE
FREDERICK DOUGLASS

FLAMEKEEPERS HAT CLUB

HARLEM

LinkNYC

125TH STREET
2 3

GINNY'S SUPPER CLUB

LinkNYC

WEST 122ND STREET

HARLEM SHAKE

SAINT NICHOLAS AVENUE
7TH AVENUE

WEST 121ST STREET

HARLEM HABERDASHERY

MANHATTAN

LinkNYC

Marcus Garvey Swimming Pool

Pelham Fritz Recreation Center

NYC Parks

Richard Rodgers Amphitheatre

WEST 120TH STREET

LinkNYC

ADAM CLAYTON POWELL JR. BOULEVARD

WEST 119TH

LENOX AVENUE

SUGAR HILL CREAMERY

Marcus Garvey Park

FIRST CORINTHIAN BAPTIST CHURCH

WEST 118TH

WEST 117TH STREET

CANAAN BAPTIST CHURCH OF CHRIST

WEST 116TH STREET

116TH STREET
2 3

LinkNYC

STREET

ADAM CLAYTON

SAINT NICHOLAS AVENUE

WEST 115TH

MALCOLM SHABAZZ HARLEM MARKET

LinkNYC

5TH AVENUE

EAST HARLEM

LinkNYC
EAST 116TH

WEST 112TH STREET

MALCOLM X BOULEVARD

Martin Luther King Playground

0   100 m

LinkNYC
EAST 115TH

LinkNYC

MADISON AVENUE

PARK AVENUE

CENTRAL PARK NORTH (110TH STREET)
2 3

Central Park

TO TASTINGS SOCIAL PRESENTS MOUNTAIN BIRD (SEE MAP LEFT)

MALCOLM X BOULEVARD
LENOX AVENUE

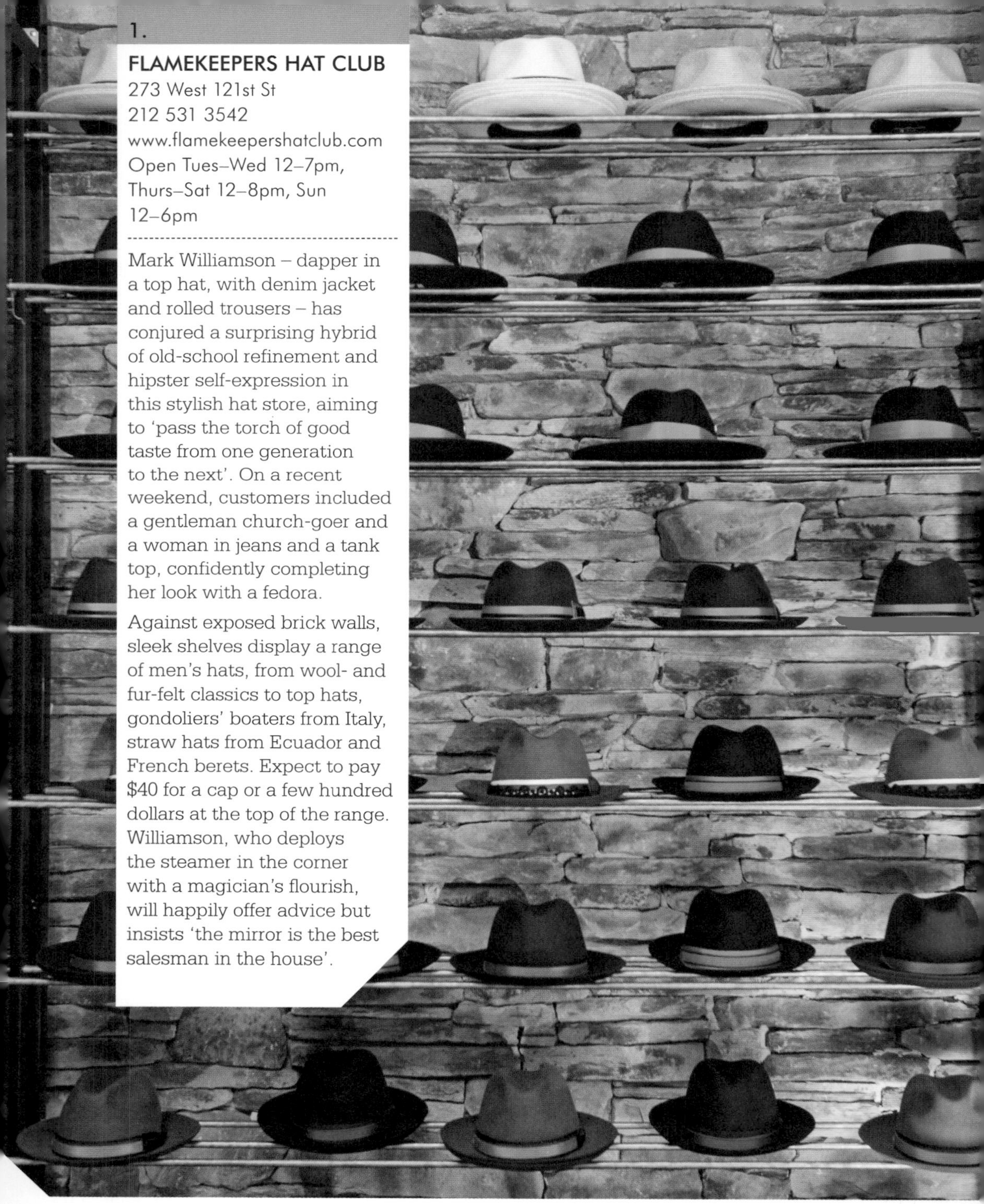

1.

FLAMEKEEPERS HAT CLUB
273 West 121st St
212 531 3542
www.flamekeepershatclub.com
Open Tues–Wed 12–7pm,
Thurs–Sat 12–8pm, Sun
12–6pm

Mark Williamson – dapper in
a top hat, with denim jacket
and rolled trousers – has
conjured a surprising hybrid
of old-school refinement and
hipster self-expression in
this stylish hat store, aiming
to 'pass the torch of good
taste from one generation
to the next'. On a recent
weekend, customers included
a gentleman church-goer and
a woman in jeans and a tank
top, confidently completing
her look with a fedora.

Against exposed brick walls,
sleek shelves display a range
of men's hats, from wool- and
fur-felt classics to top hats,
gondoliers' boaters from Italy,
straw hats from Ecuador and
French berets. Expect to pay
$40 for a cap or a few hundred
dollars at the top of the range.
Williamson, who deploys
the steamer in the corner
with a magician's flourish,
will happily offer advice but
insists 'the mirror is the best
salesman in the house'.

MALCOLM SHABAZZ HARLEM MARKET
52 West 116th St
212 987 8131
Open Mon–Sun 9am–8pm

We could be in Dakar, according to my well-travelled shopping companion, as we cruise racks of vibrant dashikis and piles of mud cloth in this sprawling market at the heart of Harlem's 'Little Senegal'. Up to 100 vendors gather daily in the semi-enclosed bazaar, selling inexpensive fashion and jewellery, baskets, masks, drums and other homewares. Score some supersized beaded earrings or a length of Dutch wax fabric.

Many merchants have similar wares, so comparison shop before parting with your cash. Sundays are quieter, which can give you an advantage in the hunt for a discount, but expect a little bit of a hard sell nonetheless – it's all part of the fun.

3.

HARLEM HABERDASHERY
245 Lenox Ave
646 707 0070
www.harlemhaberdashery.com
Open Mon–Sat 12–8pm

You could easily miss this store, tucked discreetly under a townhouse – which is how its celebrity clients like it. Once inside, this den of bling oozes unapologetic success. Guy Wood and his wife, Shay, have been dressing musicians and sports stars – think Jay-Z, Biggie, Missy Elliott, LeBron James – for more than 20 years in their custom label, 5001 Flavors. The same design sense is seen in the in-house brand of this family-run boutique, where modern American silhouettes, like motorcycle or varsity jackets, are reimagined in funky tartans or studded in gold with the store's initials. Jackets range from hundreds to a couple of thousand dollars, but you can also purchase Harlem-themed t-shirts and accessories that won't break the bank.

While you're there, press Guy on some of their famous clients, including the strange story about the last suit ever tailored for The Notorious B.I.G.

4.

SYLVIA'S
328 Malcolm X Blvd
212 996 0660
sylviasrestaurant.com
Open Mon–Sat 8am–10.30pm,
Sun 11am–8pm

The late 'Queen of Soul Food', Sylvia Woods held court at her legendary namesake restaurant until she was 80, opening it as a lunch counter in the early 1960s and nurturing it to become the 450-seat establishment that now occupies an entire block in central Harlem.

The decor, like the food, is basic and comforting. Sylvia's isn't fancy but it is fun, including a daily happy hour from 4–7pm, live music every Wednesday, unlimited mimosas at Saturday brunch, and a gospel brunch on Sundays. Don't leave without trying the Southern fried chicken (crispy on the outside and moist on the inside) or catfish, falling-from-the-bone ribs in Sylvia's 'sassy sauce', or the baked macaroni and cheese.

Yes, it's an international tourist attraction, with busloads pulling up for dinner service, but Sylvia's vibrates with history and you can't manufacture that. Skip the long lines for the gospel brunch by making a reservation.

5.

TASTINGS SOCIAL PRESENTS MOUNTAIN BIRD

251 East 110th St
212 744 4422
www.tastingsnyc.com/
mountain-bird
Open Tues–Sun 6–10pm
(dinner), Sat–Sun 12–3pm
(brunch)

Esquire gave this tiny restaurant with the overly long name the 'best new restaurant' gong in 2015, and while other reviews are uneven, the concept is intriguing and the results are mostly tasty, always creative and sometimes brilliant.

The quaint 31-seat French bistro is the vision of Japanese chef Kenichi Tajima and his wife, Keiko, who are eager to promote head-to-foot consumption of chicken and other poultry. Hence the 'bite size head to toe sampler', featuring cockscomb, heart, liver and wing; tacos made with chicken gizzard confit; cassoulet with cockscomb sausage; and ostrich tartare.

Brunch is a relatively tame affair – all the culinary wizardry takes place after dark.

6.

HARLEM SHAKE

100 West 124th St
212 222 8300
www.harlemshakenyc.com
Open Sun–Thurs 8am–11pm,
Fri–Sat 8–2am, Mon–Fri
8am–12pm (brunch), Sat–Sun
8am–2pm (brunch)

It's hard to believe this old-school burger joint, with its mid-century modern interior and devoted local following, only opened in 2013. A wall of fame displays autographed headshots from more than 200 celebrities, a 'wall of fro' showcases some of the classic hairstyles of its customers, and the theme continues in the bathrooms, decorated with hundreds of covers from *Jet* magazine (a weekly launched in the 1950s for African American readers).

Expect your typical fast-food fare ('Shake Shack, but Harlem', as a local put it), but with some exceptional Caribbean 'jerk' additions – a spicy burger and a chicken sandwich. Take the edge off the heat with a refreshing retro beverage, like the Georgette – half lemonade, half watermelon juice – or a Mexican cola.

5.

6.

6.

5.

5.

6.

7.

SUGAR HILL CREAMERY

184 Lenox Ave
212 634 9004
www.sugarhillcreamery.com
Open Mon–Sun 10am–10pm

The first thing you'll notice when you enter this bright, airy shop are the smiling portraits of people from the neighbourhood painted on the walls. The murals are by local artist Raul Ayala, and are rotated throughout the year. It's part of proprietors Nick and Petrushka Larsen's commitment to celebrating their community, which sees them also sourcing and selling Harlem-made jams and baked goods.

As well as the usual favourites (vanilla, chocolate, salted caramel), the menu features seasonal ice-cream flavours – which during an autumn visit included pumpkin spiced cheesecake, candied apple cider, and cinnamon. They also offer several vegan options, such as chocolate sorbet. The couple see themselves as part of the neighbourhood's creative lineage, and have included some throwbacks to honour the area's past – there are sundaes, a ginger beer float and a malt shake in a nod to Harlem's last soda fountain, Thomforde's, which closed in 1983.

LOCAL TIP
Sugar Hill Creamery's coffee window opens at 6.30am, serving a locally roasted African blend of Cameroon and Ethiopian coffee.

SUGAR HILL CREAMERY

GINNY'S SUPPER CLUB
310 Lenox Ave
212 421 3821
www.ginnyssupperclub.com
Open Thurs–Sat 6–10pm, Sun
10.30am–12.30pm (brunch)

- -

There's a lot of buzz around chef Marcus Samuelsson's high-profile restaurant, Red Rooster (upstairs from Ginny's), with its inventive Southern-meets-Swedish comfort food, vibrant art and raucous gospel brunches. People queue for brunch from 9am on a Sunday.

Less well known is this bar downstairs, modelled after a 1920s speakeasy and almost as secret. The look is retro chic – banquettes and white tablecloths, bathed in a warm glow – and the atmosphere is lively.

An 18-seat bar means you should always be able to slip in for a drink, some banter and live entertainment, but the tip here is to book a table and dine as well. Reservations are taken for gospel brunch, too, offering the same soul-food smorgasbord that's served upstairs along with the irrepressible energy of a local Harlem choir.

For half a century, New York's premier showcase for work by artists of African descent, as well as work influenced by black culture, has been the **Studio Museum in Harlem** (144 West 125th St). Plans for a rebuild on the existing site mean it will be on the move between 2018 and 2021, so check the website (studiomuseum.org) to discover where the collections are being shown.

Stevie Wonder, Ella Fitzgerald, Lauryn Hill and James Brown all got their start at the **Apollo Theater** (253 West 125th St), and you can still join the notoriously tough crowd there for the weekly amateur night, deciding who will 'be good or be gone'. Check the calendar, too, for dance, comedy and musical tribute nights. Or opt simply to join a tour of the historic venue, which was one of the few in New York that allowed African Americans to attend and perform when it opened in 1934.

Harlem's artistic spirit spills beyond its music venues and museums. It is celebrated in the fashion statements of its residents and the colourful, political street art that populates dozens of its walls – particularly in East Harlem, affectionately known as 'El Barrio'. **Hush Tours** hosts a wall art and graffiti tour, as well as a couple of hip-hop tours (www.hushtours.com). Or take a historical tour celebrating jazz and gospel music, or the Civil Rights movement, run by **Harlem Heritage Tours** – all led by locals raised in the neighbourhood (www.harlemheritage.com).

Tourists are welcome at the 11.30am worship service at the **Abyssinian Baptist Church** (132 West 138th St), which is world famous for its uplifting sermons, gospel choir and dance ministry. Keep in mind this is a church – not a performance space – and respect the dress code (found online) and no-camera policy. A few days of the year are kept just for regular attendees, so check the website before planning a visit. The line forms early, at the south-east corner of West 138th Street and Adam Clayton Powell Jr Boulevard. Alternatively, visit the **First Corinthian Baptist Church** (1912 Adam Clayton Powell Jr Blvd), in a historic movie palace, with a massive congregation (of almost 7000 members) and energetic services and choir; or the dynamic services at **Canaan Baptist Church of Christ** (132 West 116th St).

With its eclectic shops, waterfront markets, and creative bars and restaurants, Williamsburg has put Brooklyn on the map for international visitors. This hive of hipsters and artisans – just a quick ride from Manhattan on the L train to Bedford Ave – was once home to immigrant factory workers, but its industrial spaces have since been converted to modern apartments.

A large ultra-Orthodox Jewish community still maintains a traditional lifestyle in the south end of the sprawling neighbourhood.

Bedford Ave; Metropolitan Ave; Lorimer St

*Different station locations for different subway lines

TO MAP RIGHT (VIA METROPOLITAN AVENUE)

METROPOLITAN AVENUE

LORIMER STREET

OKONOMI

BLIND BARBER

WILLIAMSBURG

24   JUN 80T6

SHOP
1 Catbird
2 Narnia Vintage
EAT
3 Egg
4 Oddfellows Ice Cream Co.
5 Okonomi
6 Diner

EAT & DRINK
7 Maison Premiere
DRINK
8 The Ides at the Wythe Hotel

East River

Bushwick Inlet Park

NY State Parks

SMORGASBURG

East River State Park

NORTH WILLIAMSBURG

LinkNYC

LinkNYC

LinkNYC

THE IDES AT THE WYTHE HOTEL

KINFOLK 90

KINFOLK 94

BROOKLYN BREWERY

McCarren Park

NORTH 11TH

NORTH 10TH

NORTH 9TH

NORTH 8TH

STREET

WYTHE

KENT

6TH

NORTH

7TH

STREET

ARTISTS & FLEAS

BROOKLYN

BEDFORD

ODDFELLOWS ICECREAM CO.

WILLIAMSBURG

AVENUE NORTH

LinkNYC

STREET

NORTH

BEDFORD AVENUE

CATBIRD WEDDING ANNEX

METROPOLITAN

WYTHE

NORTH

5TH

4TH

BERRY

LinkNYC

NORTH

6TH

AVENUE

NORTH

3RD

EGG

LinkNYC

MAST BROTHERS CHOCOLATE

CATBIRD

DRIGGS

1ST

LinkNYC

NITEHAWK CINEMA

BEDFORD

STREET

SCOSHA

GRAND STREET

STREET

METROPOLITAN AVENUE

ROEBLING

TO OKONOMI (SEE MAP LEFT)

MAISON PREMIERE

LinkNYC

SOUTH

1ST

GRAND

NARNIA VINTAGE

LinkNYC

THE CITY RELIQUARY MUSEUM

0   100 m

N

SOUTH

BEDFORD

2ND

AVENUE

STREET

Berry Street Garden

SOUTH

3RD

Espiritu Tierra Community Garden

SOUTH

BERRY

SOUTH

4TH

DRIGGS

ROEBLING

SOUTH

1ST

HAVEMEYER

STREET

MARCY

AVENUE

RANDOLPH BEER

SOUTH

5TH

STREET

PIES 'N' THIGHS

WILLIAMSBURG   BRIDGE

DINER

BROADWAY

1.

CATBIRD

219 Bedford Ave
718 599 3457
www.catbirdnyc.com
Open Mon–Fri 12–8pm,
Sat 11am–7pm, Sun 12–6pm

The star attraction of this tiny store is a tiny ring – fashioned from gold and half a millimetre wide. The 'threadbare ring' costs less than $50, but the shop's stackable-rings specialty is designed to be highly addictive, and weekend crowds attest to this. This and other covetable day-to-day pieces – like Catbird's personalisable charms and first-knuckle rings – are designed in-house, and are sold alongside items from designers like Pamela Love, Sofia Zakia and Nancy Kraskin. The boutique also carries a well-edited range of home products and stationery, including its signature Neighbor's Fig Tree candles – an ode to Brooklyn's abundant trees, with a suggested reading list of classic New York stories tucked inside the box. Catbird's associated **Wedding Annexe** around the corner (540 Driggs Ave) sells non-traditional rings by local designers, takes inspiration from bohemian couples such as Serge Gainsbourg and Jane Birkin, and aims to be 'dude friendly'.

2.

NARNIA VINTAGE

672 Driggs Ave
718 781 4617
narniavintage.com
Open Mon–Sun 11am–7pm

Otherworldly by name and by nature, Narnia Vintage is a dreamy space – uncrowded, yet full of bohemian, one-of-a-kind treasures waiting to be discovered during a leisurely browse. Proprietor Molly Spaulding painted the floor herself – it depicts phases of the moon – as well as a motif of rainbow stripes that flows down the wall, creating the perfect backdrop for colour-blocked garments that span 100 years of fashion.

The sales desk is set towards the rear of two rooms separated by curtains, and there are no overbearing sales pitches or sense of surveillance – just the opportunity to explore a range of '80s sequins, '70s Lanvin pantsuits and finely embroidered Chinese jackets alongside vintage Afghan pendants and leather belts, plus a glass cabinet of crystals.

The fact that everything feels like a precious find is not reflected in the prices, which range from under $50 into the hundreds, for rare and designer labels.

LOCAL TIP

Lovers of indie jewellery should also seek out **Scosha** (64 Grand St) and, on weekends, the **Artists and Fleas** market (70 North 7th St).

1.

2.

1.

3.

EGG

109 North 3rd St
718 302 5151
www.eggrestaurant.com
Open Mon 7am–5pm, Tues
7am–3pm, Wed–Fri 7am–5pm,
Sat–Sun 8am–5pm

- -

Williamsburg's play-hard lifestyle drives a demand for restorative morning meals, and the success of this local favourite proves that a restaurant can be taken seriously even without a dinner sitting. According to owner George Weld, the all-day breakfast venue – which has a second outpost in Tokyo – adheres to an uncomplicated ethos: simple food, cooked perfectly from good ingredients. The eggs Rothko is a crowd favourite – a thick slice of brioche with an egg cooked in its middle, covered in a blanket of creamy, melted Vermont cheddar. Fresh-baked buttermilk biscuits are accompanied by gravy or sweet condiments, or – on the lunch menu – by fried chicken. Sandwiches feature indulgent fillings, like fried oysters, pulled pork or seared duck breast and duck liver pâté, but it's the all-day breakfast that has won hearts for over a decade now.

LOCAL TIP
For all-day Southern comfort favourites, from chicken and waffles to banana cream pie, head to **Pies 'n' Thighs** (166 South 4th St).

4.

ODDFELLOWS ICE CREAM CO.

175 Kent Ave
347 599 0556
www.oddfellowsnyc.com
Open Sun–Thurs 12–11pm,
Fri–Sat 12pm–12am

Don't be fooled by the old-school appearance of this 20-seat ice-cream parlour – a nostalgic confection of wooden stools, a chalkboard menu and candy-striped walls. Its rotating selection of 12 flavours is 100 per cent futuristic, and includes chorizo caramel swirl, cornbread, purple rice, edamame, and caramelised onion – all of which can also be spun into sodas or thick shakes. In an archive that now numbers more than 300 flavours, from peanut butter and jelly to foie gras, only one was ever deemed too odd even for OddFellows and retired from the list: coconut curry.

5.

OKONOMI
150 Ainslie St
www.okonomibk.com
Open Mon–Tues & Thurs–Fri
9am–3pm, Sat–Sun 10am–
4pm; Yuji Ramen Mon–Tues &
Thurs–Fri 6–11pm; Okonomi
Omakase Sat from 8pm

Miraculously, this 12-seater manages to be three restaurants in one – Okonomi, Yuji Ramen and a Saturday night Omakase sitting. The speciality here is ichiju sansai – a traditional Japanese set meal of a soup and three side dishes, for breakfast or lunch, made up of rice, miso, soup, pickled vegetables, a choice of fish and a couple of petite sides. For a little extra, you can (and should) add an onsen egg – poached and floating in a sauce of sake and soy, to stir through your rice. The ramen-based dinner menu changes daily. For either meal, line up outside and leave your contact details, while the lucky dozen inside dine in peace. On weekends, you can face a one- to two-hour wait. Reservations are taken (a month in advance is recommended) for the Saturday night 8-course Omakase ('I'll leave it up to you') meal – a $140 exercise in pure trust, that features local seafood and seasonal vegetables, and closes with a special tea preparation.

DINER
85 Broadway
718 846 3077
dinernyc.com
Open Mon–Thurs 6pm–12am,
Fri 11–12am, Sat–Sun 10–12am

The flavourful grass-fed beef burgers are a staple at Diner, but the rest of the menu here changes daily, testing the memories of the good-natured waiters. In a fun bit of dining theatre, the server will write out the day's specials tableside on a piece of paper, also sitting with you (room permitting) to explain what's what. Dishes might include rabbit spaetzle or lamb meatballs in the winter, or a peach-and-tomato panzanella in the summer.

This funky venue is housed inside a 1920s train carriage, miraculously managing to offer booth, table and bar seating as well as outdoor dining options.

Opened in 1999, Diner is credited as the first of the hip, farm-focused New American restaurants that now flourish in Brooklyn. Culinary superstar owner Andrew Tarlow now oversees an impressive empire, which includes the beloved **Marlow and Sons** next door (81 Broadway), with a great oyster offering and a daily-changing menu, as well as **The Ides** (see p. 164) and **Reynard** in the Wythe Hotel, among others.

7.

MAISON PREMIERE

298 Bedford Ave
347 335 0446
maisonpremiere.com
Open Mon–Thurs 2pm–2am,
Fri 2pm–4am, Sat 11–4am,
Sun 11am–4pm

Capturing the spirit of Belle
Époque Paris and the French
Quarter of New Orleans,
Maison Premiere revels in
the twin pleasures of oysters
and absinthe. It has a list of
more than 30 of the former,
and serves New York City's
largest selection of premium
absinthes. It's a spirit best
enjoyed by slow-dripping
ice water over a sugar
cube, but there's also an
absinthe-centric cocktail
list and other options for
those not romanced by the
green fairy. Centre stage,
dispensing water, is a marble
replica of a famous absinthe
fountain, topped with a
jaunty statuette of Napoleon
Bonaparte, that once graced
a bar in New Orleans. All of
the action takes place in an
elegant two-roomed 'salon',
dominated by a horseshoe-
shaped bar, and in the shady,
pebbled courtyard out the
back – utterly seductive and
very date-worthy. Oyster
happy hour ($1 apiece) runs
Monday to Friday from 4pm
to 7pm, and from 11am until
1pm on weekends.

8.

THE IDES AT THE WYTHE HOTEL

80 Wythe Ave
718 460 8006
wythehotel.com/the-ides
Open Mon–Thurs 4pm–
12.30am, Fri 2pm–1.30am,
Sat 12pm–1.30am, Sun
12pm–12.30am

The indoor-outdoor Ides bar
has a party vibe and a killer
view. The outlook from the
terrace on the 6th floor of the
hip Wythe Hotel is especially
good from sunset, when
the sweeping Manhattan
skyline takes on a dramatic
hue before shading to that
quintessential New York
silhouette – iconic buildings
and bridges illuminated
with glittering lights. With
the view-plus-terrace
combination, the Ides can
get very crowded in the
warm months, resulting
in queues at ground level
and staggered progress
to the roof. After 6pm on
Friday and Saturday nights
there is a $10 card-only
cover charge, which you
can skip by reserving an
indoor table. While the
breathtaking outlook is truly
the main attraction, the
cocktails are dependable (if
pricey), there is a small-plate
menu available, and the
establishment is blessedly
tip-free.

7.

7.

8.

7.

7.

7.

WHILE YOU'RE HERE

Williamsburg is a food lovers' mecca as well as an epicentre for artisan manufacturers, providing some wonderful options to get close to food producers.

Harking back to a time when the area was a hub of beer brewing, the **Brooklyn Brewery** (79 North 11th St) not only manufactures and serves from its brewhouse and tasting room, but offers tours of the facilities. Book for a mid-week small brewery tour with tastings, or just turn up for free general tours on weekends.

Courtesy of Roald Dahl's bestselling 1964 novel, pretty much everyone under the age of 50 harbours a fantasy of getting behind the scenes at a chocolate factory. **Mast Brothers Chocolate** (111 North 3rd St) runs public tours daily, guiding visitors through bean-to-bar production and the stories behind its celebrated packaging.

On Saturdays from April to October, you can sample food from more than 100 vendors at the massive open-air food market on the waterfront, **Smorgasburg** (90 Kent Ave). Novelties might include spaghetti 'donuts', fruit that is juiced inside itself and drunk from its shell, or Dutch stroopwafels, made on the spot.

Nitehawk Cinema (136 Metropolitan Ave) shows a reliably savvy selection of new indie as well as retro films, but the fun is in the in-theatre meals and drinks service – including themed menu items to match the movie. Every feature is preceded by a specially produced supercut of scenes from rare and classic films that touch on similar themes to the main event.

What began as a quirky display in a downstairs apartment window has evolved into the **City Reliquary Museum** (370 Metropolitan Ave). This odd, hole-in-the-wall mini-museum is packed with New York City artefacts, including memorabilia from New York World's Fairs, a salvaged mid-century paper stand, and 'a set of antique dentures, washed ashore at Dead Horse Bay'. Members of the public lend beloved objects for display in the touching Community Collections section.

As well as fostering hybrid careers, this neighbourhood embraces genre-defying spaces, like **Blind Barber** (524 Lorimer St), a barber shop that is also a cafe and full bar; **Kinfolk** (90 and 94 Wythe Ave), a store that functions as a cafe, bar, gallery and nightspot, with a groovy interior build

inspired by geodesic domes; and **Brooklyn Bowl** (61 Wythe Ave), a live music venue, bowling alley and restaurant rolled into one.

Just north of Williamsburg is the more low-key – but equally hip – Greenpoint. The former industrial precinct, known as New York's 'Little Poland', has in recent years become a hub for artists and innovative food and fashion. The result is a comfortable mix of traditional Polish bakeries alongside sleek cocktail bars, and churches acting as pick-up points for farm-produce schemes.

Greenpoint's waterfront location at the northernmost point of Brooklyn adds to the village-like atmosphere, making it perfect to explore.

 Greenpoint Ave; Nassau Ave

*Different station locations for different subway lines

Map labels

TO MAP RIGHT (VIA FRANKLIN STREET)

LinkNYC

HOUSE OF VANS

NORTHERN TERRITORY

LinkNYC

NASSAU AVENUE

FIVE LEAVES

TØRST

KINFOLK 90 & 94

BROOKLYN BREWERY

McCarren Park

FOX AND FAWN

NYC Parks

BEDFORD AVENUE

GREENPOINT

Streets: ST, CALYER, LEONARD, ECKFORD, AVENUE, STREET, LORIMER, GUERNSEY, MESEROLE, STREET, MANHATTAN, STREET, FRANKLIN STREET, DOBBIN, STREET, NORMAN AVENUE, AVENUE, STREET, AVENUE, WYTHE, AVENUE, NASSAU, AVENUE, BEDFORD, AVENUE, NORTH, 11TH, NORTH, 10TH, STREET, STREET

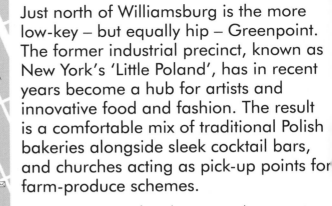

24   JUN 2016

SHOP
1 FRANKLIN STREET
2 BELLOCQ TEA ATELIER

EAT
3 FIVE LEAVES
4 BAKERI
5 GLASSERIE
6 MILK AND ROSES

17

DRINK
7 TØRST
8 NORTHERN TERRITORY

GLASSERIE ○

BOX STREET

Newtown Creek

COMMERCIAL STREET

LinkNYC 🛜

CLAY STREET

○ MILK AND ROSES

Greenpoint Playground

DUPONT STREET

GREENPOINT

MANHATTAN

N

EAGLE STREET

LinkNYC 🛜

WEST

FRANKLIN

BAKERI ○

STREET

FREEMAN

STREET

0   100 m

GREEN

LinkNYC 🛜

AVENUE

BROOKLYN

STREET

STREET

LinkNYC 🛜

STREET

HURON

STREET

INDIA

INDIA STREET

STREET

⊕ GREENPOINT

JAVA

⊕ WOLVES WITHIN

BELLOCQ TEA ATELIER

KENT STREET

HOME OF THE BRAVE

GREENPOINT AVENUE Ⓖ

○

GREENPOINT

AVENUE

🚇

OVENLY BAKERY

⊕ IN GOD WE TRUST

BROOKLYN NIGHT BAZAAR ⊕

⊕ WNYC TRANSMITTER PARK

ADAPTATIONS ⊕

⊕ ALTER

East River

WEST

PAS MAL ⊕

SUNSHINE LAUNDROMAT ⊕

American Playground

⊕ WORD

STREET

NOBLE STREET

NOBLE STREET

TO NORTHERN TERRITORY, FIVE LEAVES & TØRST (SEE MAP LEFT) ↓

OAK STREET

STREET

OAK STREET

CALYER

169

1.

FRANKLIN STREET

The quiet haven of Franklin Street has a concentration of indie boutiques and stores offering books, homewares and fashion – much of it locally designed and made.

Wolves Within (no. 174) was established in 2011 by husband-and-wife duo Max and Bethany Vogel, both art directors, to sell carefully curated, American-made clothing and accessories. Three years later, they opened **Home of the Brave** (no. 146), offering a range of ceramics, blankets, kitchenware and stationery that mixes Brooklyn makers with global artisans.

Alter (no. 140) specialises in easily wearable, chic and structural fashions for men and women, with a neutral spectrum. The staff are helpful with styling the pieces.

Word (no. 126) is a small store that knows its audience, with an inventory inspired by the community – a lot of paperback fiction, especially classics, plus cookbooks and stationery. The shop also acts as a social hub, hosting book groups and readings, and running a book lovers' basketball league.

Across the road, **Pas Mal** (no. 99) has an even more restrained palette than Alter, exuding understated good taste and Scandinavian austerity.

Adaptations (no. 109) is sweetly arranged like a home, so you can imagine just how nice its mid-century knick-knacks, rugs, housewares and furniture would look in your own place.

Find more well-curated fashion, including a jewellery collection made on-site, around the corner at **In God We Trust** (70 Greenpoint Ave).

BELLOCQ TEA ATELIER

104 West St
347 463 9231
www.bellocq.com
Open Wed–Thurs 12–6pm,
Fri–Sat 12–7pm, Sun 12–5pm

Tea is surely one of the simplest comforts and loveliest gifts, evoking memories of places and people with each brew. This petite Bellocq 'atelier' in a nondescript industrial pocket of Greenpoint is a surprise, with rows of beautifully packaged teas – some rare, with prices to match – displayed in bright yellow canisters against Venetian plaster walls. Find single-estate teas sold whole leaf, organic tea and herbal blends assembled on-site, as well as a range of candles inspired by the in-house concoctions. My pilgrimage of many years to replace a discontinued favourite tea ended happily here with the discovery of Kiyuka, a blend of Japanese sencha with rose essence and petals. Another fragrant treat is the White Nixon – a blend of white peony tea, lavender and grapefruit – to drink iced or in a cocktail in the summer.

3.

FIVE LEAVES

18 Bedford Ave
718 383 5345
fiveleavesny.com
Open Mon–Sun 8–1am

This relaxed restaurant with an Australian vibe and a nautical theme has been a neighbourhood favourite since it opened in 2008, co-founded by late actor Heath Ledger. Open from breakfast till after midnight – and even featuring an 'in between' menu to bridge the moments between meals – it attracts a steady crowd, often meaning a wait at the bar given its 'no reservations' policy.

Australians will be nostalgic at the comfortingly good coffee, avocado toast, rosewater pavlova and a burger that includes grilled pineapple, pickled beetroot and a fried egg. The wait for a seat on weekends is notoriously long, but take heart – the brunch menu, including ricotta pancakes with honeycomb butter, berries and maple syrup, is offered seven days, and well into the afternoon.

Spoil yourself with a very on-trend Turmeric Bees Knees gin-based cocktail – it's almost a health drink.

4.

BAKERI

105 Freeman St
718 349 1542
www.bakeribrooklyn.com
Open Mon–Fri 7am–7pm,
Sat–Sun 8am–7pm

There is an instant feeling of wellbeing in this Greenpoint outpost of Bakeri, with its long communal table, riot of giant plant life on the Nathalie Lété wallpaper and, of course, its tasty baked goods. When Norwegian Nina Brondmo opened the original Bakeri in nearby Williamsburg, its small-batch European-style bread and cosy styling made it an instant – and crowded – success. This larger version tucked away on a residential side street is more efficient but still homely, from the salvaged fixtures to the vintage-style uniforms and hand-lettered signs in the pastry case. It's a nice place for lunch or to find a snack, with vegan and gluten-free options available.

For something out of the ordinary, seek out the traditional Scandinavian skolebrød, a Norwegian sweet roll with custard and grated coconut.

4.

4.

3.

3.

3.

4.

5.

GLASSERIE

96 Commercial St
718 389 0640
www.glasserienyc.com
Open Mon–Thurs 11.30am–
2.30pm & 5.30–11pm,
Fri 11.30am–2.30pm &
5.30pm–12am, Sat 10am–
4pm & 5.30pm–12am, Sun
10am–4pm & 5.30–11pm

In a rustic 1860 glassworks at the northernmost point of the Brooklyn waterfront, founding chef Sarah Kramer and owner Sara Conklin have woven Middle Eastern and Mediterranean family influences into a menu crafted from locally sourced produce. Kramer left in 2014, but their respective Israeli and Lebanese heritages are evident in dishes such as harissa lamb, chicken kibbe and the wildly popular flaky bread, while spices including saffron, cardamom and turmeric have even snuck into the cocktails.

Sharing is encouraged, especially at brunch – every bit as special as dinner – when the whole table is invited to participate in a flat-rate meze feast. It's a bit of a trek to get to, but its relative isolation and proximity to the water enhance the ambience.

MILK AND ROSES

1110 Manhattan Ave
718 389 0160
milkandrosesbk.com
Open Mon–Thurs 10am–11pm,
Fri–Sat 10–12am, Sun 10am–
10pm (kitchen closes an hour
earlier each day)

Milk and Roses features two quite different, strikingly beautiful spaces. The street-facing restaurant has the look of an old library, with book-lined shelves, a dark wood bar, pressed metal ceilings and red leather banquettes. But walk through the back door and you'll come upon a lush garden, with rustic furnishings, flowerbeds, and mirrors whimsically hung around the walls.

In both spaces, the thoughtful menu, with a southern Italian influence, will have you marvelling at the freshness and flavours of the ingredients – from the harvest salad to the panna cotta. If you're looking to indulge yourself during the day, a prix fixe menu includes unlimited mimosas.

Come prepared, as all transactions are cash only and it's quite a walk to a bank.

7.

TØRST

615 Manhattan Ave
718 389 6034
www.torstnyc.com
Open Sun–Thurs 12pm–12am,
Fri–Sat 12pm–2am

This sleek, wood-panelled bar aims to satisfy even the most earnest beer devotee, with its 21 constantly rotating taps and more than 200 bottled beers – some of them rare ones. It's the brainchild of Jeppe Jarnit-Bjergsø – the 'gypsy brewer' behind Denmark's Evil Twin – and Daniel Burns, who has worked at Noma and Momofuku labs.

Tørst also offers up a beer-friendly food menu, divided simply into sandwiches, snacks and share food. As deceptively plain as it sounds, many punters return for the addictive bread plate – a crusty sourdough served hot with butter.

Beer aficionados will appreciate the venue's custom-built draught system that allows individual lines to be set to the optimal temperature and gas blend. For everyone else – come for a drink recommended by an expert, and receive a gentle education.

8.

NORTHERN TERRITORY

12 Franklin St
347 689 4065
www.northernterritorybk.com
Open Mon–Tues (summer only), Wed–Fri 5pm–close, Sat–Sun 11am–close

----

This Australian-themed bar comes into its own in the warm months, when its expansive rooftop and laid-back summer vibe make it an excellent place to watch the sun set behind the city skyline.

The casual menu is faux global – sometimes all in the same dish, as with the bánh mì tacos – satisfying, and not expensive. It's classic pub food. Snack on a meat pie made by Australian purveyor Tuck Shop, or fill up on a huge 'Aussie beef burger' as you gaze across the East River at the Empire State Building, lit a different colour every night.

Australian, New Zealand and domestic beers are all available on tap – and with an optional shot.

7.

8.

Brooklyn Night Bazaar
(150 Greenpoint Ave) is a
combined karaoke, ping pong,
mini golf and arcade complex, plus
an indoor market of 50 vendors,
selling jewelry, vintage clothes and
vinyl, all in a historic banquet hall
in the heart of Greenpoint.

If you love the arcade games at
the Night Bazaar, then head across
the road to **Sunshine Laundromat**
(860 Manhattan Ave). Past the
classic pinball machines at the
front, and washing machines at
the back – as you'd expect in a
laundromat – you'll find a bar and
full pinball parlour, including some
rare vintage games and a chimp
automaton in a glass case who'll
tell you your fortune for a quarter.

Pick up a peanut butter cookie or
a piece of Brooklyn blackout cake
from the proudly women-owned

Ovenly bakery (31 Greenpoint
Ave) and take in the million-dollar
view of the Manhattan skyline
from **WNYC Transmitter Park**. The
2.6 hectare (6.4 acre) park was
once the home of the WNYC radio
transmission towers and has been
repurposed as a green space,
where you can also see films
screened in summer.

It's only a 6-minute walk from
here to the India Street stop on
the East River Ferry – joining the
neighbourhood to Manhattan in
midtown (34th Street) at one end
and Wall Street at the other, with
stops in between on the Brooklyn
side in Williamsburg and DUMBO.

Time seems to have stood still at
the **Peter Pan Donut and Pastry
Shop** (727 Manhattan Ave),
with an interior that dates back
to the 1950s. From 4.30am

on weekdays (a little later on weekends), waitresses in retro uniforms serve up a wide variety of old-fashioned donuts, cakes and bagels, plus milkshakes and that Brooklyn specialty, egg creams (see p.234). Grab a treat and head over to nearby **McCarren Park**, which straddles both Green Point and Williamsburg. A popular hangout for locals and families, this 4000 square metre (35 acre) park has plenty of recreational facilities, including baseball field, soccer fields, basketball courts, running track and even an outdoor pool that's a designated historic landmark.

Music-lovers should check out nearby **Warsaw**, an 800-person capacity music venue located in an old polish community centre. The acoustics in this former ballroom can apparently be a bit touch and go, but visitors can chow down on polish favourites like kielbasa and blintzes while they listen to acts. Find out about upcoming events via their website (www.warsawconcerts.com).

Gutter Bowling Alley and Bar (200 North 14th Street) is a wicked combo of eight-lane bowling alley and dive bar. A calendar of events (www.thegutterbrooklyn.com) includes rock bands on weekends, comedy acts and animation screenings, but any night of the week you can order a pitcher of beer and play pool in the main room, or bowl in the side room.

Bushwick is perched on the precipice between gentrification and grungy old New York. A decade ago, struggling artists turned Williamsburg and Greenpoint into hipster havens. Now the lure of lower rents and undiscovered industrial spaces has imbued Bushwick with a similar appeal, bringing exciting music venues, bars, vintage shopping and creative spaces.

The tsunami of urban renewal and sub-cultural migration has united the creative energies of young professionals with international music, food and languages, that makes Bushwick the perfect place to experience old and new New York at its best.

 Morgan Ave; Jefferson St; Knickerbocker Ave

*Different station locations for different subway lines

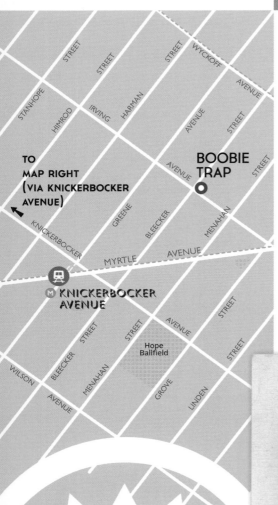

BUSHWICK

24   JUN 8016

SHOP
1 FRIENDS
2 URBAN JUNGLE
3 CATLAND
4 BETTER THAN JAM
EAT
5 ROBERTA'S
6 ICHIRAN

17

EAT & DRINK
7 SYNDICATED
DRINK
8 BOOBIE TRAP

TO MAP RIGHT (VIA KNICKERBOCKER AVENUE)

BOOBIE TRAP

KNICKERBOCKER AVENUE

Hope Ballfield

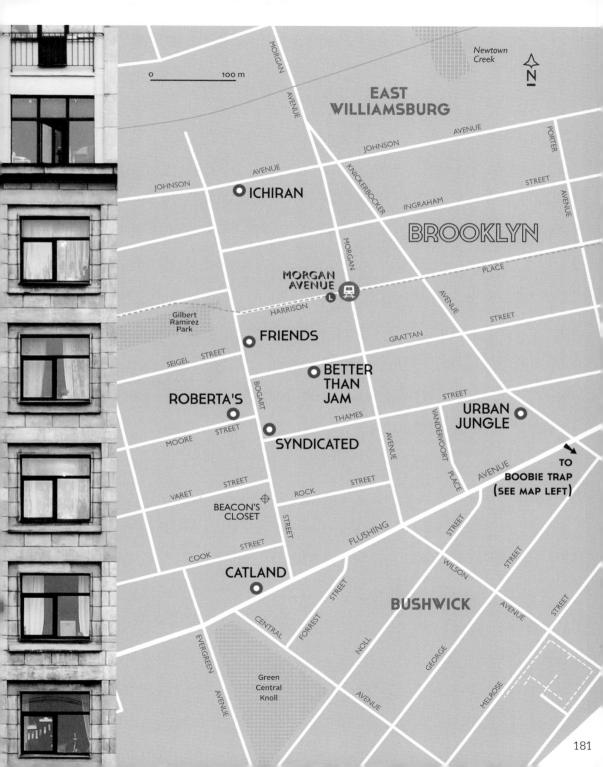

1.

FRIENDS

56 Bogart St
718 386 6279
www.shopfriendsnyc.com/
#home-section
Open Mon–Sun 11am–8.30pm

- -

Friends is a self-proclaimed indie department store with a simple mission: 'to bring super cute clothing, shoes, and accessories at super cute prices to one and all'. Opened by fashion designer BFFs Mary Meyer and Emma Kadar-Penner in 2012, this Bushwick basement is loaded with contemporary and vintage fashion, handmade shoes and sandals, ridiculously cute oversized glasses, beard grooming kits, gifts and novelties. Embracing the Brooklyn maker market, they champion local products and New York labels like Lila Rice and Floss Gloss.

With 204 square metres (2200 square feet) of goodies to explore, there's plenty of papercrafts, home decor and unique pieces to fatten up the suitcase.

LOCAL TIP

You can easily make a day of Bushwick's vintage stores by visiting **28 Scott** (28 Scott Ave), **Worship** (117 Wilson Ave), **Fox & Fawn** (570 Manhattan Ave) and **Beacon's Closet** (23 Bogart St), a consignment store full of quality fashion pieces.

URBAN JUNGLE
118 Knickerbocker St
718 381 8510
https://ltrainvintage.com/pages/
urban-jungle
Open Mon–Sun 12–8pm

Urban Jungle is a larger-than-life vintage store nestled among abandoned warehouses and vibrant street art. A thrift superstore at heart, it's filled to the brim with 1950s cabaret gowns, army surplus, worn Levis, cowboy boots and much more. You can get lost for hours on end in its over-stocked racks. Beyond the bountiful supply of fashionable ephemera, there are hundreds of unique antiques hanging from above or stacked in any spare hutch or shelf. Discovering early Mickey Mouse phones, vintage guitar amps and plaster Laurel and Hardy statues (which are sadly not for sale) will make the place enticing even for those with no interest in second-hand shopping.

3.

CATLAND

987 Flushing Ave
718 418 9393
www.catlandbooks.com
Open Sun–Thurs 12–8pm,
Fri–Sat 12–9pm

Catland is a metaphysical bookshop and a cabinet of curiosities for people looking for the esoteric, the spiritual and the bewitching. It's one of the few places you can go in Bushwick that offers both reading matter and the opportunity to get a reading from its in-house clairvoyants.

Entering through thick velvet curtains, you'll find the atmosphere is dark and cozy and the air thick with sandalwood incense. Refurbished wooden tables house bouquets of dried herbs, cedar branches and other mystical botanicals. Floor-to-ceiling shelves and hutches house everything from dusty copies of Aleister Crowley's *The Nature of the Beast* to decks of oracle and tarot cards to shiny new tomes on paganism, the occult, Wiccan, and astrology. Browse saucers of polished precious stones, crystal runes and pewter pendants or sample the rich aromas of essential oils and incense. Catland even offers introductory classes on tarot reading and Wiccan 101 sessions.

BETTER THAN JAM
20 Grattan St
929 441 9596
www.betterthanjamnyc.com
Open Fri–Mon 1–6pm

To truly fit in the hipster haven that is Bushwick, you may need to look the part. At Better than Jam, you can definitely find the goods to 'go local'. Part store, part workshop and part public studio space, this designer co-op sells handmade products from locally based designers, some of whom even create their own unique lines in-house, including a selection of clothing, jewellery and other accessories. The store has a DIY feel, with basic shelving units, whitewashed walls and wire racks used to display all manner of unique textiles, ceramics and designs.

There's no doubt a trip here will have you feeling inspired to create something of your own, so it is just as well they offer regular workshops in dyeing, screen printing and crafting for all experience levels. Spaces are limited so make sure to reserve your seat online.

ROBERTA'S

261 Moore St
718 417 1118
www.robertaspizza.com
Open Mon–Fri 11–12am,
Sat–Sun 10–12am

New Yorkers are fiercely protective of their favourite pizza spots and Roberta's is one of these well-guarded secrets. Hidden behind graffiti-covered corrugated iron walls is a tiki-themed beer garden, bar and one of NYC's best and hippest pizzerias, with a shipping container dining room. Entering via a simple screen door, you'll pass under the oh-so-eighties Roland keytar synth hanging above the Roberta's sign, and be greeted by a pleasing aroma of onions, pepperoni and cheese, straight out of the wood-fired oven.

In summer, expect a 30-minute wait closer to dinner, but luckily it's easy to get a drink to pass the time and before you know it, you'll be seated in the shipping container, listening to Roberta's own food radio station broadcasting from the rear. The perfectly executed margherita should be mandatory for every diner, or try local favourite in name and flavour, the Hawt Gabagool (the Jersey Italian for Capicola, this pie brings together mozzarella, taleggio, house coppa, garlic, basil, giardineira and lemon).

ICHIRAN

374 Johnson Ave
718 381 0491
en.ichiran.com
Open Sun–Thurs 11am–
10.30pm, Fri–Sat 11am–
11.30pm

You know a place does something well when it's the only thing on the menu. Slurping down salty pork ramen is more than just a guilty pleasure, and the ramen at Ichiran is next level. Here, you can concentrate on its deep flavours in quiet contemplation, at what looks remarkably like a library study desk (with the addition of screens that can be drawn up for your food to be passed through from the kitchen). It's a perfectly anonymous place to avoid awkward conversations and slurp noisily, but for those who prefer dining together, Instagramming food and discussing the flavours, a full dining room with group seating is also available.

Ichiran Ramen lets you choose how salty you want it, how spicy, the softness of the ramen noodles, how much pork you want and requisite extras like an egg or seaweed, which instead of being shredded, is presented as sheets on a separate plate. The result? You'll spend the rest of your existence trying to find ramen this good.

7.

SYNDICATED

40 Bogart St
718 386 3399
syndicatedbk.com
Open Mon–Wed 5pm–12am,
Thurs 5pm–3am, Fri 5pm–2am,
Sat 3pm–2am, Sun 3pm–12am

Art house meets alehouse at Syndicated, a Bogart Street mainstay that brings together cocktails, craft brews, burgers and the best new screenings from local independent filmmakers and classic independent movies, in its own cinema.

From the outside, it gives nothing away. It could be just like any bar on this strip. Inside, its style evokes the golden era of cinema with Art Deco typefaces on the directional signage, simple but comfortable furnishings and an ornate bar dressed with banker's lamps. Towards the back of the venue, through soundproof doors is the small dine-in theatrette that seats 60 people. Book online to secure a seat – especially for cult classics. Not only can you enjoy cinema treats like salty popcorn, the house burgers are just as traditional and delightful. Try the seasonal cocktails (named after different movies) or enjoy an adult version of a chocolate milkshake, spiked with chilli-infused tequila.

8.

BOOBIE TRAP

308 Bleecker St
347 240 9105
www.boobietrapbrooklyn.com
Open Mon–Sat 12pm–4am,
Sun 12pm–12am

When it comes to hipster hangs, the Boobie Trap is a top-heavy, kitsch-heavy dive bar. From the moment you enter, you will be greeted by friendly staff. There's a naked torso with twin beer taps as its ovaries and a blackboard loaded with dirt-cheap drink specials. The tunes are edgy-cool, mostly '70s punk and early-'80s New Wave, and the crowd is generally creative types in their late 20s to early 40s.

Each table has a classic game like Monopoly or Scrabble under a layer of glass, laminated board games or you can battle it out over a competitive game of Hungry Hungry Hippos. The decor is a mish-mash of styles: fish tanks with floating breast toys, 1950s B-movie nostalgia, vintage toys, and titillating topless burlesque posters punctuated by humorously crass, attitude-heavy, in-your-face slogans. That good humour extends to its drink specials, with cheeky cocktails like That Time of the Rumth and a free drink if you present a freshly cut-off man-bun.

8.

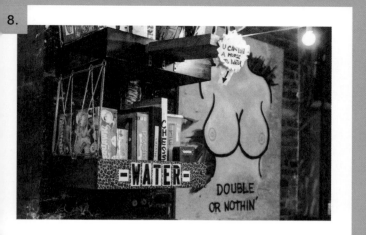

8.

7.

7.

7.

8.

Charge up your smart phone or have your DSLR camera at the ready, because Bushwick is a precinct perfect for street photography. Wander around what were once industrial wastelands to find quirky hole-in-the-wall shops or hidden bars and venues around the Jefferson L stop and take in the endless array of murals and graffiti in the side streets off Knickerbocker Avenue.

Open all year round, the **Bushwick Collective** (Troutman St at Saint Nicholas Ave) is an open-air 'gallery' that displays artwork from some of the city's greatest street artists, who have transformed the crumbling walls of rusting warehouses into colourful canvasses. If you're lucky, you might even catch the artists in action.

Cottage crafts and the handmade spirit extends to drink offerings in the area. Stop by **Kings County Brewers Collective** (381 Troutman St), which offers a large selection of locally brewed craft beers available on tab and bottled.

The Nobel Experiment (23 Meadow St), named after the nickname given to Prohibition, is a small batch distillery owned and operated by Brooklyn native, Bridget Firtle. The birthplace of Owney's white rum, only available in eight U.S. states, offers tours on Friday afternoons at 3pm.

For the sweet tooth, be sure to check out **Fine & Raw Chocolate** (288 Siegel St), handmade by Brooklyn artist Daniel Sklaar. Organic, sustainable and plant-based, the chocolates are made in small batches on the premises. The labels are in themselves works of art, and the factory doubles as a gallery and art space.

The **Bushwick Starr** (207 Starr St) is a great place to see up-and-coming theatre performers. The not-for-profit theatre fosters neighbourhood talent and emerging artists, and hosts a full slate of local productions. Check out the website (thebushwickstarr.org) to find out about upcoming shows.

For those looking to experience the local party scene, **House of Yes** (2 Wyckoff Ave) takes theme to the extreme by frequently hosting variety shows, discos and era dance parties. Tickets are occasionally available at the door, but it's best to book ahead (houseofyes.org). What happens in the House of Yes … well, you know how that ends.

Fort Greene and Clinton Hill are adjacent Brooklyn communities that have weathered the ups and downs of great wealth and deep poverty, and in recent decades become a significant cultural precinct with a vibrant culinary scene. Streetscapes of stately brownstones and townhouses are home to intimate dining spaces and artisanal boutiques.

Bedford–Stuyvesant (Bed-Stuy) has taken longer to be revitalised, and retains an appealingly high-spirited edge. Its diverse mix of residents means Caribbean fast food joints, brisket bars and Southern grills rub shoulders with innovative craft beer joints and artisan doughnut bakeries.

Atlantic Ave–Barclays Center; Clinton–Washington Aves; Utica Ave
*Different station locations for different subway lines

Map labels:
JEFFERSON
LEWIS
AVENUE
STUYVESANT
STREET
HANCOCK
SARAGHINA
HALSEY
STREET
SARAGHINA BAKERY
BAR LUNÀTICO
MACON
AVENUE
STREET
MACON STREET
LEWIS
MACDONOUGH
STREET
DECATUR
STREET
TO MAP RIGHT (VIA FULTON STREET)
BAINBRIDGE
AVENUE
LinkNYC
Fulton Park
UTICA AVENUE
A C
FULTON
STREET
HERKIMER
STREET
ATLANTIC
AVENUE
AVENUE

24   JUN 2016

SHOP
1 LEISURE LIFE NYC
2 GREENLIGHT BOOKSTORE

EAT
3 SISTERS
4 LOCANDA VINI E OLII
5 SARAGHINA
6 WALTER'S AND KARASU
DRINK
7 BAR LUNÀTICO

FORT GREENE, CLINTON HILL & BED-STUY

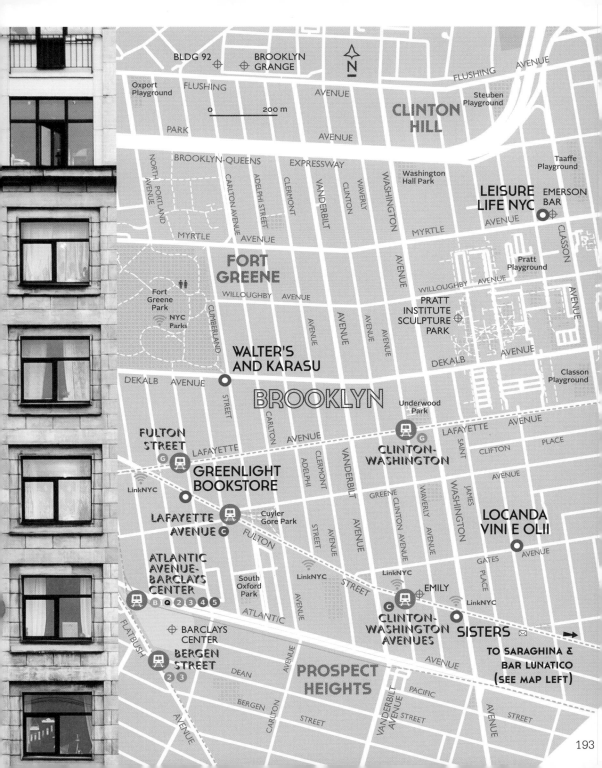

BLDG 92
BROOKLYN GRANGE

Oxport Playground
FLUSHING
FLUSHING AVENUE
FLUSHING AVENUE

Steuben Playground

N

0   200 m

PARK AVENUE

AVENUE

CLINTON HILL

BROOKLYN-QUEENS EXPRESSWAY

NORTH PORTLAND AVENUE
CARLTON AVENUE
ADELPHI STREET
CLERMONT
VANDERBILT
CLINTON
WAVERLY
WASHINGTON

Washington Hall Park

Taaffe Playground

LEISURE LIFE NYC
EMERSON BAR

AVENUE

CLASSON AVENUE

MYRTLE AVENUE
MYRTLE
AVENUE

Pratt Playground

FORT GREENE

Fort Greene Park
NYC Parks

WILLOUGHBY AVENUE
WILLOUGHBY AVENUE

PRATT INSTITUTE SCULPTURE PARK

CUMBERLAND
AVENUE
AVENUE
AVENUE
AVENUE

AVENUE

WALTER'S AND KARASU

DEKALB AVENUE

DEKALB AVENUE

Classon Playground

BROOKLYN

STREET
CARLTON
AVENUE

Underwood Park

LAFAYETTE AVENUE

FULTON STREET
G

LAFAYETTE
CLERMONT
ADELPHI

VANDERBILT

G CLINTON-WASHINGTON

SAINT

CLIFTON PLACE

JAMES

AVENUE

GREENLIGHT BOOKSTORE

LinkNYC

GREENE AVENUE
CLINTON AVENUE
WAVERLY AVENUE
WASHINGTON

LOCANDA VINI E OLII

LAFAYETTE AVENUE
C

Cuyler Gore Park

FULTON

STREET
AVENUE
AVENUE

GATES PLACE
AVENUE

ATLANTIC AVENUE-BARCLAYS CENTER
B Q 2 3 4 5

South Oxford Park

LinkNYC

LinkNYC

C CLINTON-WASHINGTON AVENUES
EMILY
LinkNYC

BARCLAYS CENTER

ATLANTIC

SISTERS

FLATBUSH

BERGEN STREET
2 3

DEAN

AVENUE
AVENUE

PROSPECT HEIGHTS

PACIFIC

TO SARAGHINA & BAR LUNATICO (SEE MAP LEFT)

VANDERBILT AVENUE
STREET

AVENUE

STREET

BERGEN

CARLTON
STREET

AVENUE

1.

LEISURE LIFE NYC

559 Myrtle Ave, Clinton Hill
347 725 3167
www.leisurelifenyc.com
Open Tues–Thurs 12–8pm,
Fri–Sat 12–9pm, Sun 1–6pm

With whip-smart curation, Charnier Corey has established a community of menswear designers and their fans. Loyal customers gravitate to the store, where the space is designed to seduce people into hanging around – big leather armchairs encourage conversation while you consider the eclectic mix of artwork and designer and vintage clothing.

The store's eponymous line takes familiar athletic silhouettes, such as baseball caps and varsity jackets, and elevates the materials (think tweed and Italian leather) to conjure a kind of modern dandy with street smarts – hip-hop inspired and aspirational.

LOCAL TIP

Emerson Bar next door (561 Myrtle Ave) holds a weekly ping-pong tournament, exhibits local artists' work and offers a different drinks special nightly.

GREENLIGHT BOOKSTORE

686 Fulton St, Fort Greene
718 246 0200
www.greenlightbookstore.com
Open Mon–Sun 10am–10pm

The broad selection in this pristine, light-filled bookshop reflects the surrounding community – progressive, literate and hyper-local. Staff picks are displayed with thoughtful reviews and an offer of 15 per cent off.

Inside the front window, a long shelf is covered in coffee-table books and children's books about New York. Beside this is a table piled high with books by the city's many authors – including Emma Straub, James Baldwin, Jonathan Lethem and Hanya Yanagihara. One section of the shop is given over to works from independent presses, a rack by the front door is filled with arts and literary magazines, and a display near the counter is devoted to the pressing issues of the times – race, feminism, democracy and resistance.

This well-loved community hub is also a good place to hear authors discuss their work, or to come for book signings. Hillary Clinton had fans around the block when she included the store on her *What Happened* book tour.

3.

SISTERS

900 Fulton St, Clinton Hill
347 763 2537
www.sistersbklyn.com
Open Mon–Fri 8–2am,
Sat–Sun 10.30–2am

Sisters can be a little 'form over function' but, if you value design and like your dining experiences Instagram-worthy, then this space will definitely appeal. The main room is dominated by a skylight, 10 metres (32.8 feet) up, whose geometric panes are echoed in the monumental wooden bar, the floor tiling and even the logo.

The simple lunch and dinner menus change seasonally, and focus mostly on snacks and shared dishes using organic and locally sourced ingredients, with a handful of larger options ('a bit more') at dinnertime.

At night, the back room becomes a live music venue or hosts a DJ, and transforms to a livelier bar and place to hang out.

LOCAL TIP
Many locals also enjoy Sisters' bar as a good place to wait for a table to come up at the small, intimate and acclaimed **Emily** pizzeria, directly across the road (919 Fulton St).

4.

LOCANDA VINI E OLII

129 Gates Ave, Clinton Hill
718 622 9202
www.locandany.com
Open Mon–Thurs 5.30–
10.15pm, Fri–Sat 5.30–11pm,
Sun 5.30–9.45pm

Although this Tuscan-influenced restaurant has been trading to positive reviews for almost 20 years, it has the appealing ambience of a 'well-kept secret'. This is due in part to its suburban location, and also its confusing signage that still reads 'Lewis Drug Store'. The lovingly re-purposed 19th century apothecary – with penny-tile flooring and original wooden cabinetry – is co-owned by its first chef, Michele Baldacci, along with sommelier Rocco Spagnardi and former waiter Michael Schall. Baldacci's rustic Florentine menu features a diverse list of antipasti and primi ingredients, including tripe and wild boar, and main dishes like braised rabbit with olives and beans, or branzino 'al cartoccio' (cooked in a paper bag). Spagnardi – whose list draws on the many rare and indigenous grapes of Italy – is committed to low mark-ups and ensures the wine selections are as much a drawcard as the food. Reservations are recommended for the small space.

LOCAL TIP

The burgeoning Saraghina family also boasts an artisanal bakery (433 Halsey St), selling fresh pastries, Italian loaves made from organic flours, and serious espresso.

SARAGHINA

435 Halsey St, Bed-Stuy
718 574 0010
www.saraghina.com
Open Mon–Fri 8am–4pm
& 5.30–11pm, Sat–Sun
10am–11pm

When Saraghina was new, it had no phone and didn't take reservations, focusing instead on building a loyal local clientele. These days, customers go out of their way to eat here and the friendly trattoria – serving blistered Neapolitan-style pizza straight from a wood-fired oven – is so popular, it has expanded into a space next door to create a tapas bar. This also offers patrons a place to drink while waiting for a table.

While the simple pizza menu offers reliable classics on a beautifully puffed crust, the specials menu of salads, antipasti, pasta and seafood changes daily.

6.

WALTER'S

166 Dekalb Ave, Fort Greene
718 488 7800
https://walterfoods.com/walters
Open Mon–Thurs 11–12am,
Fri 11–1am, Sat 9–1am,
Sun 9–12am

KARASU

347 223 4811
www.karasubk.com
Open Sun–Thurs 5.30–11pm,
Fri–Sat 5.30pm–12am

With its pleasant outlook on
Fort Greene Park and serving
every kind of drop-in meal –
from brunch to cocktails
and oysters – Walter's has
a winning combination of
friendly service, old-time
decor and well-executed
classics, like fried chicken
with mashed potatoes and
gravy, watermelon salad,
and catfish sandwiches. The
sun-filled diner takes on a
romantic hue at night, as
the leather banquettes and
cherry wood bar are bathed in
the golden light of tungsten
bulbs. If you don't land a table
for dinner, keep walking.
A door in the back leads to
Karasu: a discreet, low-key
'izakaya' with a smooth jazz
soundtrack. Small share plates
with a seasonal focus are
served alongside sake, shochu
and Japanese whisky, plus
meticulously crafted cocktails
with a Far Eastern inflection,
like the Daydream – white
rum, Nigori sake, green tea
and coconut.

7.

BAR LUNÀTICO

486 Halsey St, Bed-Stuy
718 513 0339
www.barlunatico.com
Open Mon–Wed 8.30–
12.30am, Thurs–Sat 8.30–
1.30am, Sun 11am–5pm

'Liquid Love', announces
the blue-and-red sign that
runs the length of this
narrow bar-cum-cafe, in
a luminous declaration
of its mezcal-inspired,
freewheeling atmosphere.
A small stage at the back
welcomes an eclectic range
of musicians – from Africa,
Latin America and the
Middle East, and every kind
of jazz performer – nightly
from 8.30pm, except on
Sundays, when a gospel
performance kicks off at 2pm
to accompany brunch. It's
an intimate space, so show
up early if you aim to make a
night of it. The exotic cocktail
menu (an Oaxacan negroni,
for example, replaces gin
and Campari with mezcal
and amari) and adventurous
menu – elk meatballs,
chilli-salt grasshoppers –
elevate Bar LunÀtico's
magical atmosphere. If
that leaves you in need of
a kickstart, LunÀtico has a
coffee happy hour, every
day except Sunday, from
8.30am to 9.30am.

7.

6.

6.

7.

7.

6.

The **Brooklyn Academy of Music** (BAM, 30 Lafayette Ave) was established in 1861 in a beautiful Beaux Arts building. BAM now also operates two additional performance spaces, in the nearby **Harvey Theater** (651 Fulton St) and **Fisher Building** (321 Ashland Pl). Distinguished by its program of edgy theatre, music and contemporary dance works, BAM also runs an art-house cinema and hosts live readings and interviews. From September to December, the **Next Wave Festival** offers a wide range of works and talks at very low prices.

If the weather is nice and you feel like stretching your legs, there are several great options in these neighbourhoods. **Pratt Institute** (200 Willoughby Ave) incorporates a sculpture park across its 10-hectare campus. More than 70 works by well-known and emerging artists are on display, including some by faculty members and graduates of the venerated art institution.

A short walk downhill from Pratt Institute is the **Brooklyn Navy Yard** – a 121-hectare (299 acre) site that was established in 1801 as one of the US Navy's first shipyards and is now home to an industrial park. **BLDG 92** tells its history in an on-site, three-floor museum that includes an interactive timeline tracking the yard's transformation since 1600. Buy a sandwich from the museum's cafe and enjoy an overview of the yard from the roof deck, or tour it by bus or bike. **Brooklyn Grange** operates a rooftop farm at the Navy Yard, offering ticketed tours on Wednesdays between May and October.

Take a stroll along Clinton Avenue, between Myrtle Avenue and Gates Avenue, to take in the grand 19th century Italianate mansions of Clinton Hill. No fewer than four of them (at 229, 232, 241 and 245) were commissioned by oil baron Charles Pratt, for himself and as wedding gifts for his three sons.

Fort Greene Park is rich in historical significance. It is Brooklyn's oldest park, and was originally the site of a fort (first in 1776, then again in 1812). A 45-metre (147-foot) monument remembers the more than 11,000 martyrs who died on British warships in nearby Wallabout Bay during the Revolutionary War. Some of their remains are buried in a crypt beneath it.

The beautiful, hilly park includes a running loop, playgrounds and tennis courts. For a picnic on the fly, there is a greenmarket every Saturday at the park's south-east corner, or drop by the all-vegan **Clementine Bakery** (299 Greene Ave) or artisan doughnut store **Dough** (448 Lafayette Ave).

Park Slope is one of Brooklyn's best-kept secrets, a quiet haven home to a multi-cultural population of young professionals and their families. Renovated brownstones line leafy, wide streets, with cosy cafes. The area is alive with summer music festivals, family-friendly restaurants, unique dining experiences and bars.

Prospect Heights boasts the Barclays Center (see p. 214), a world-class sports and concert venue, and plenty of quality restaurants and bars to stop by en route to Prospect Park (see p. 214). Cross the park to vibey Crown Heights with its artists, galleries, cute cafes and energetic bars.

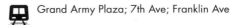 Grand Army Plaza; 7th Ave; Franklin Ave

*Different station locations for different subway lines

PARK SLOPE, PROSPECT HEIGHTS & CROWN HEIGHTS

24   JUN 8016

SHOP
1 Brooklyn Superhero Supply Company
2 Norman and Jules
3 Marche Rue Dix

17

EAT
4 The Chocolate Room
5 Olmsted
6 Talde
7 Chavela's
DRINK
8 Butter & Scotch

ATLANTIC TERMINAL

B D N Q R 2 3 4 5

ATLANTIC AVENUE-
BARCLAYS CENTER

D N R

ATLANTIC
AVENUE-
BARCLAYS
CENTER

B Q 2 3 4 5

FULTON

CLINTON
HILL

LinkNYC STREET

C

EMILY

CLINTON-
WASHINGTON
AVENUES

ATLANTIC

AVENUE

WASHINGTON

AVENUE

LinkNYC

BARCLAYS
CENTER

BERGEN
STREET

2 3

DEAN

PROSPECT
HEIGHTS

STREET

THE
CHOCOLATE
ROOM

LinkNYC

FLATBUSH

SAINT
MARKS

AVENUE

LinkNYC

LinkNYC

PARK
SLOPE

5TH

AVENUE

6TH

AVENUE

7TH

AVENUE

B Q

PARK

AVENUE

VANDERBILT

AVENUE

STERLING

AVENUE

OLMSTED

PLACE

PLACE

EASTERN
PARKWAY-
BROOKLYN
MUSEUM

R

UNION
STREET

LinkNYC

LinkNYC

UNION
HALL

AVENUE

AVENUE

PRESIDENT

STREET

7TH

GRAND
ARMY
PLAZA

2 3

SOLDIERS'
AND SAILORS'
ARCH

FLATBUSH

EASTERN PKWY

Mount
Prospect
Park

2 3

BROOKLYN
MUSEUM

OLD
STONE
HOUSE

LinkNYC

2ND

3RD

5TH

6TH

GARFIELD

STREET

STREET

STREET

STREET

GRAND
ARMY
PLAZA
GREENMARKET

PLACE

8TH

TO BUTTER & SCOTCH,
MARCHE RUE DIX
& CHAVELA'S
(SEE MAP LEFT)

BROOKLYN
SUPERHERO
SUPPLY
COMPANY

NORMAN
AND
JULES

BROOKLYN

AVENUE

5TH

STREET

WEST

AVENUE

Long
Meadow

AVENUE

BROOKLYN
BOTANIC
GARDEN

BARBÈS

7TH
AVENUE

F G

AVENUE

6TH

7TH

9TH

STREET

STREET

STREET

STREET

PARK

NYC
Parks

Prospect
Park
Zoo

TALDE

7TH

10TH

11TH

12TH

AVENUE

STREET

STREET

PROSPECT

NYC Parks
BANDSHELL

15TH STREET-
PROSPECT
PARK

F G

14TH STREET

16TH

STREET

8TH

STREET

STREET

N

Prospect
Park
Lake

The
Nethermead

NYC
Parks

0   200 m

3RD

BERGEN

BALTIC

BUTLER

DOUGLASS

4TH

AVENUE

STREET

STREET

STREET

STREET

STREET

UNION

1.

BROOKLYN SUPERHERO SUPPLY COMPANY

372 5th Ave, Park Slope
718 499 9884
www.superherosupplies.com
Open Mon–Sun 11am–5pm

Where do Gotham's heroes go for their costumes and creative writing inspiration? This quirky retailer is as much a store for masks, capes and crime fighting weapons as it is a secret lair for imaginative young minds. Crossing the threshold is like stepping onto the set of the original 1960s *Batman* series with a capery displaying colourful satin cape options for any ensemble. Between rows of metal shelving you can peer through the portal to the secret command centre – a library and creative writing studio, where local authors and uni students volunteer to offer tutoring, support and even publishing services for young writers. Access to this creative lair is through a secret bookcase and it is regularly booked for kids' parties. Other highlights include a mind-reading machine and a de-villainiser.

All of the novelties, toys and merchandise purchased raise funds for the creative writing program, with the store and program staffed by kind-hearted volunteers.

NORMAN AND JULES
158 Seventh Ave, Park Slope
347 987 3323
www.normanandjules.com
Open Mon–Sat 9am–7pm,
Sun 10am–6pm

Park Slope's old world charm comes to life in this oh-so-cute toy store that reinvents simple, handcrafted, sustainable and traditional toy designs for a new generation. The owners of Norman and Jules have found a unique niche in the market supported by a local community that values quality and design sensibilities.

Browsing the store is like a trip down memory lane. Beautifully painted wooden figures and puzzles in bright, modern pantone colours line the shelves, next to abstract hand-sewn dolls with outfits so adorable you will be wishing they were in your size. To inspire imaginative play, budding orienteers can pick up a treasure finding kit, and future engineers can learn a thing or two about gears with moving dioramas and puzzles. There's also plenty of tasteful and pastel nursery decor that is sure to melt your heart.

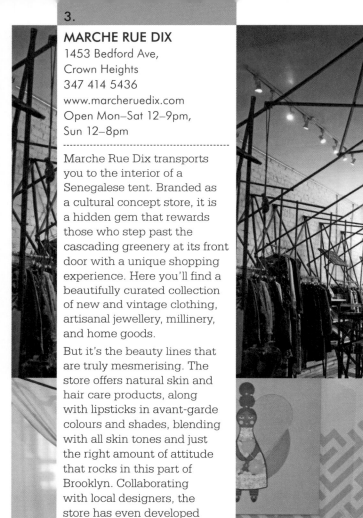

3.

MARCHE RUE DIX
1453 Bedford Ave,
Crown Heights
347 414 5436
www.marcheruedix.com
Open Mon–Sat 12–9pm,
Sun 12–8pm

- -

Marche Rue Dix transports
you to the interior of a
Senegalese tent. Branded as
a cultural concept store, it is
a hidden gem that rewards
those who step past the
cascading greenery at its front
door with a unique shopping
experience. Here you'll find a
beautifully curated collection
of new and vintage clothing,
artisanal jewellery, millinery,
and home goods.

But it's the beauty lines that
are truly mesmerising. The
store offers natural skin and
hair care products, along
with lipsticks in avant-garde
colours and shades, blending
with all skin tones and just
the right amount of attitude
that rocks in this part of
Brooklyn. Collaborating
with local designers, the
store has even developed
12 shades of small-batch
branded nail colours that are
truly unique. Take home the
store's own textile-and-body
spray 'Dakar', with notes of
amber musk, rose, lavender,
patchouli and nutmeg.

LOCAL TIP
Try **Café Rue Dix** next
door, which locals declare
as having the best burgers
in Brooklyn.

THE CHOCOLATE ROOM

51 5th Ave, Park Slope
718 783 2900
thechocolateroombrooklyn.com
Open Sun–Thurs 12–11pm,
Fri–Sat 12pm–12am

This is a dessert cafe made for people who like their chocolate on chocolate with a side of chocolate. It has built a reputation among locals as a place of decadence and indulgence, serving up steaming, hot mugs of specialty cocoa blends and homemade sweets.

The setting is unique, with dark marbled tabletops juxtaposed against exposed brick walls, honeycombed tiles and simple glassware accents that are a nod to Brooklyn's ice-cream parlours of yesteryear.

While the treats on offer can be enjoyed all day long, I recommend going in the evening as nothing beats a candle-lit dessert and glass of wine to decompress after a day exploring the city. The chocolate brownie is a crowd pleaser for all ages, but a treat for the adults is the black chocolate stout float, made with Brooklyn Brewery's chocolate stout and a scoop of the Chocolate Room's homemade vanilla ice-cream.

Take the goodness home with a jar of their homemade sauces or cocoa blends.

5.

OLMSTED

659 Vanderbilt Ave,
Prospect Heights
718 552 2610
www.olmstednyc.com
Open Mon–Sun 5–10.30pm

Forget farm to table, Olmsted sources much of its fresh produce from its lush back garden and this is reflected on every plate with a seasonal, ingredient-driven menu that places vegetables in the spotlight.

It's named after Frederick Law Olmsted, the landscape architect responsible for designing nearby Prospect Park as well as Central Park and San Fran's Golden Gate Park.

Each delectable dish is presented like a work of art that is easily on par with Manhattan's finest establishments with green, leafy garnishes, colourful edible petals and even light foams.

The 50-seat restaurant's interior blends natural recycled wood tables and industrial cast-iron accents with natural elements like a vibrant living wall. Out the back, enjoy refreshing cocktails in the tiny garden – a rarity for most New Yorkers.

Reservations are recommended but Mondays are reserved for walk-ins.

TALDE

369 Seventh Ave, Park Slope
347 916 0031
www.taldebrooklyn.com
Open Mon–Wed 5–11pm,
Thurs–Fri 5pm–12am, Sat
11am–3pm & 5pm–12am,
Sun 11am–3pm & 5–11pm

Asian fusion is at its most extreme at Talde, where a worldly and seasonal menu is served in portions that can be enjoyed solo or shared. Seat yourself in a casual booth and admire the charming old-world bar where a lucky cat waves its right arm in welcome, presided over by an ever-watchful Chinese dragon.

The restaurant's executive chef, Dale Talde, is a regular on reality shows such as *Top Chef*, which has driven traffic through the doors since 2012, but it's the locals who fill the place for most dinners and through the brunch rush. Try the arroz caldo, a Filipino inspired dish consisting of rice-pudding-like soup that is bursting with fresh ginger, garlic and tiny tender chunks of chicken. The dumpling is the restaurant's stalwart – salty sausage meat encased in thick, crunchy layers of pretzel dough dipped in some super-hot mustard. And if you like the food, you can take it home with you in the form of Talde's self-titled cookbook.

7.

CHAVELA'S

736 Franklin Ave, Crown Heights
718 622 3100
www.chavelasnyc.com
Open Mon–Thurs 11am–11pm,
Fri 11–12am, Sat 10–12am, Sun
10am–11pm

Chavela's is a fun and sexy Mexican eatery and a popular local go-to for brunch or date nights that won't break the bank. When entering the colourful cantina-inspired venue, your eyes will dart between the hand-painted tiles adorning the walls, and the beautifully crafted dark wood bar.

With a fresh (and possibly original) take, the queso fundito is great to share with friends, with a melted white queso cheese covering black beans and sautéed green peppers, alongside sauces you wish you could bottle and take home. For a more traditional dish, the mole here is second to none, with the creamy chocolaty sauce generously poured over half a chicken served with traditional rice and beans.

The impressive selection of regional mescals and tequilas stacked high on the shelf will mean you don't know where to start. Possibly with the house-made margaritas and sangrias until you move onto the hard stuff (because you can afford to here).

In the warmer months, dine outside and bask in the sun.

8.

BUTTER & SCOTCH

818 Franklin Ave, Crown Heights
347 350 8899
www.butterandscotch.com
Open Mon 5pm–12am,
Tue–Thurs 9–12am, Fri 9–2am,
Sat 10–2am, Sun 10–12am

This popular feminist-themed dessert and cocktail bar will draw you in from the street with its smell of freshly baked pies, and inside there are cute neon signs spruiking 'eat cake', vibrant coloured walls and kitschy accessories.

Local baking identities Keavy Blueher and Allison Kave ran a Kickstarter campaign in 2013 that raised the funds to launch this bar and they haven't looked back.

The menu is a riot, with drinks named after old-school feminist slogans and woman warriors – I'll have a 'Samantha Jones', please! Unique boozy shakes (try the pina colada) or milk-based cocktails are paired with tasty treats such as the white Russian and salted chocolate chip cookie. But I'd suggest upgrading to a unicorn treat, a sugar cookie with colourful sprinkles and edible glitter for those who love a little sparkle.

7.

8.

LOCAL TIP
Butter & Scotch's merchandise includes cookbooks and trademarked jars of #bitcheslovesprinkles. And where else can you drink for a cause? From each cocktail, $1 is donated to charitable causes like Planned Parenthood.

Prospect Park (bordered by Prospect Park West, Southwest and Ocean Ave) is a must-see at all times of the year. There is public access to many sporting fields (when not in use by amateur athletic leagues), skating rinks, barbecues and free classes such as yoga. In summer, the park comes alive during the **Celebrate Brooklyn** festival, with free concerts from big name acts in the **Band Shell**. You can even traverse the park on horseback by renting your four-legged companion for the day from nearby **Kensington Stables** (51 Caton Pl). And don't miss the impressive triumphal **Soldier's and Sailor's Arch** at Grand Army Plaza, which borders the park.

Grand Army Plaza Greenmarket (Prospect Park West and Flatbush Ave) operates every Saturday as a one-stop organic, fresh-from-the-farm shop. You can also pick up specialty meats, homemade pies and treats, and gawk at the varieties of locally grown flowers for sale, which also make for great Instagram inspo.

For fans of live music and big sporting events, the **Barclays Center** (620 Atlantic Ave) plays host to the Brooklyn Nets (basketball), Long Island Islanders (ice hockey), WrestleMania and a packed calendar of premium touring acts. It's a more affordable alternative to Madison Square Garden if you want a taste of American sport.

Brooklyn Museum (200 Eastern Parkway) has an outstanding collection of worldly and decorative arts that spans five floors, and frequently hosts an array of cultural events like yoga classes and salsa parties. Plan ahead as it is closed on Mondays and Tuesdays.

Before they relocated to LA, the Dodgers were Brooklyn's favourite baseball team. The **Old Stone House** (336 3rd St, open Fri–Sun) located in Washington Park was their first club house. It now serves as a small museum offering visitors the chance to learn of the Battle of Brooklyn in the American Revolution.

Brooklyn Botanic Garden (1000 Washington Ave) is beautiful and should not be missed, even when not during its peak cherry blossom season in April. With numerous themed gardens, including the children's garden and tropical glasshouses, this is the perfect spot to pack a picnic and relax pond-side.

The **Brooklyn Children's Museum** (145 Brooklyn Ave) is budget friendly (especially on Thursdays, 2–6pm, when it offers a pay-as-you-wish fee), and will keep curious young minds busy with interactive exhibits including a sensory room, block lab and seasonal offerings such as a wilderness camp.

If you're looking for a fun night out, the area is packed with unique venues that cater to all interests. Drop by **Barbes** (376 9th St) for a taste of Paris circa the 1980s. The bar offers readings, screenings and world music performances in its low key and almost dive-bar like environment. **Union Hall** (702 Union St) stages regular comedy nights, '90s singalongs and an indoor bocce league. Its interior is styled like a stately home, complete with fireplace and library. Its sister venue, **The Bell House** (149 7th St) completes the round-up with a club/live music venue vibe and a full calendar of events year-round.

FRONT
GENERAL
STORE

JOHN   STREET

PLYMOUTH   STREET

WATER   STREET

BURROW
FRONT   STREET   VINEGAR
HILL
HOUSE

BERL'S BROOKLYN
POETRY SHOP

YORK
STREET   YORK   STREET

PROSPECT STREET

RANDOLPH
BEER   ← TO MAP RIGHT
(VIA PROSPECT   SANDS   STREET
& HENRY STREETS)

Trinity
Park   NASSAU   STREET

CONCORD   STREET

TILLARY   STREET

JAY ST

BRIDGE   STREET

GOLD   STREET

FLATBUSH   AVENUE   EXTENSION

BROOKLYN-QUEENS EXPRESSWAY

JAY

STREET

BROOKLYN
HEIGHTS &
DUMBO

Across Brooklyn Bridge from the city, two
neighbourhoods are joined by **Brooklyn
Bridge Park** (see p.226), with striking
views of Manhattan. Wealthy Brooklyn
Heights is characterised by its historic
churches, elevated promenade and
beautiful streetscapes. Once a bohemian
outpost of artists and writers, it now has
luxury development on the waterfront and
piers reclaimed for public recreation.

Dumbo (Down Under the Manhattan Bridge
Overpass) is a hip community of tech start-ups,
restaurants and independent stores occupying
former factories and lofts.

 Borough Hall; Clark St; York St

*Different station locations for different subway lines

24   JUN 8016

SHOP
1 FRONT GENERAL *S*TORE
2 GOOSE BARNACLE
EAT
3 COLONIE
4 BURROW
5 VINEGAR HILL HOUSE

17

DRINK
6 INTERSECTION OF HENRY *S*T
AND ATLANTIC AVE

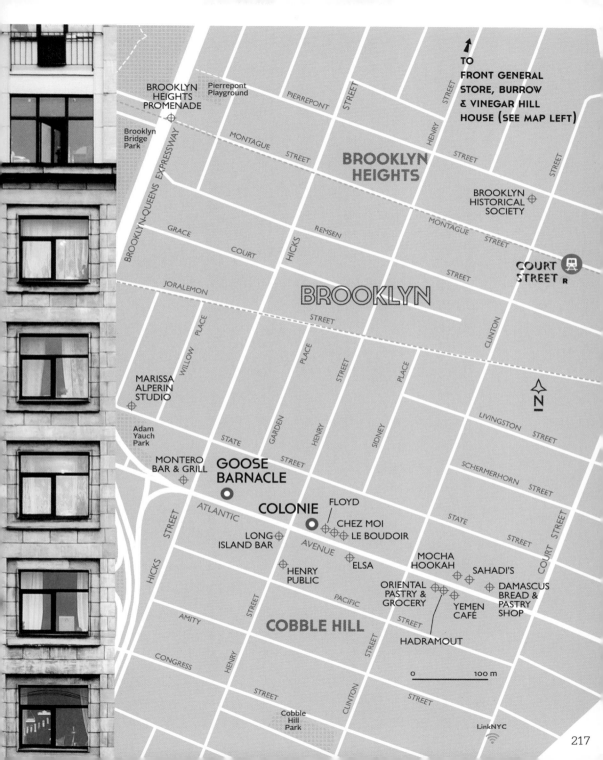

BROOKLYN
HEIGHTS
PROMENADE

Pierrepont
Playground

PIERREPONT STREET

HENRY STREET

STREET

TO
FRONT GENERAL
STORE, BURROW
& VINEGAR HILL
HOUSE (SEE MAP LEFT)

Brooklyn
Bridge
Park

MONTAGUE STREET

BROOKLYN
HEIGHTS

BROOKLYN-QUEENS EXPRESSWAY

GRACE

COURT

HICKS

REMSEN

MONTAGUE STREET

BROOKLYN HISTORICAL SOCIETY

STREET

COURT
STREET R

JORALEMON

BROOKLYN

STREET

WILLOW PLACE

PLACE

STREET

PLACE

CLINTON

N

MARISSA
ALPERIN
STUDIO

Adam
Yauch
Park

GARDEN

HENRY

SIDNEY

LIVINGSTON STREET

STATE

STREET

SCHERMERHORN STREET

MONTERO
BAR & GRILL

GOOSE
BARNACLE

ATLANTIC

COLONIE

FLOYD

CHEZ MOI
LE BOUDOIR

STATE STREET

COURT STREET

LONG
ISLAND BAR

AVENUE

ELSA

MOCHA
HOOKAH

SAHADI'S

HICKS STREET

HENRY
PUBLIC

PACIFIC

ORIENTAL
PASTRY &
GROCERY

YEMEN
CAFÉ

DAMASCUS
BREAD &
PASTRY
SHOP

AMITY

HENRY

STREET

COBBLE HILL

STREET

HADRAMOUT

CLINTON

0   100 m

CONGRESS

STREET

Cobble
Hill
Park

STREET

LinkNYC

217

1.

FRONT GENERAL STORE

143 Front St, Dumbo
646 573 0123
www.frontgeneralstore.com
Open Mon–Sat 11.30am–
7.30pm, Sun 11.30am–6.30pm

In keeping with the frontier spirit of Dumbo, this store is inspired by the old trading posts of the south-west. Owner Hideya Sagawa has mixed vintage Americana with wares from Japan and a great collection of mid-century European sunglasses in a deep space that invites hands-on exploration.

Walls, counters and even the ceiling are adorned with hand-picked treasures – from vintage sweatshirts and Navajo jewellery to felt football pennants. New kimonos hang alongside vintage Levi's; shelves display beautifully detailed men's brogues, piles of fisherman's caps and dapper Borsalinos.

There is also a wide range of well-priced, easily packed handmade ceramics and other keepsakes.

GOOSE BARNACLE

91 Atlantic Ave,
Brooklyn Heights
718 855 2694
www.goosebarnacle.com
Open Tues–Sun 11am–7pm

One of the first things you'll notice in David Alperin's high-end-casual menswear store are the old telephone booths, repurposed to display gloves, ties and baseball caps. They came from his grandmother's 1950s-era Long Island Bar across the street and are a nod to Alperin's longstanding roots as a fourth-generation Brooklyn native.

While he has a hyper-local service ethos, noting regulars' sizes and preferences for future recommendations, the former private banker also has a sharp, global sensibility – selling Svensson jeans from Sweden, Fred Perry sportswear from Britain and Journal shirts from Denmark, as well as articles from Thailand and Japan, and New York's own Malin+Goetz skincare products. He's also a soccer tragic and sells the jersey he designed for his local 'middle-aged dads' team (Goose Barnacle Football Club) in amongst the Assembly t-shirts – noting that the jersey has since been absorbed into the street swag of the local teens.

LOCAL TIP

David's sister sells delicate jewellery set with colourful gems at **Marissa Alperin Studio** (25 State St), in a nearby side street.

3.
COLONIE

127 Atlantic Ave,
Brooklyn Heights
718 855 7500
www.colonienyc.com
Open Mon–Thurs 5.30pm–
12am, Fri 5.30pm–1am,
Sat 11–1am, Sun 11–12am

There's usually a wait at this
local favourite but you can
pull up a stool at the lively
bar beneath the vertical
garden until a table becomes
available. Unless you're with
a larger group, opt to dine
at the chef's bar, where you
can watch the food being
fearlessly prepared over
leaping flames.

The seasonal menu sources
ingredients from local
farms as much as possible
and the menu format
is unconventional and
fun – divided into categories
that include snacks, cheese,
vegetables, pasta, and 'small'
and 'large'. Most dishes
are suitable for sharing and
there's a good selection
for vegetarians.

The menu changes quarterly,
but a few smaller, signature
items remain constant for a
reason (they're delicious).
These include ricotta and
honey crostini, and warm
doughnuts with Meyer lemon
and thyme sugar.

4.
BURROW

68 Jay St, Dumbo
www.burrow.nyc
Open Mon–Fri 9am–4pm

Tucked at the far end of
an office building lobby,
the tiny shop and atelier of
pastry chef and food artist
Ayako Kurokawa is hard to
find but worth the effort. If
you're lucky, you'll see some
of her special-order portrait
cookies or sculptural cakes,
but even her daily creations
are masterpieces, like her
pastry resembling a plait,
or shortcake moulded and
painted to mimic a peach.

Kurokawa's pastries are
based on classic French
recipes – caramel-edged
far bretons, crunchy and
buttery gateaux basques,
but incorporate both
Japanese and American
influences – think black
sesame and roasted green tea
in cookies, and walnut-based
cheesecake that is whipped
full of air, like a souffle.

Only breakfast items are
available when the store
opens; cookies and cakes
appear from around 10.30am,
with noon being the peak
time to find the biggest
variety of baked goods.

Kurokawa was previously
pastry chef at the Modern
(Danny Meyer's MoMA
restaurant) as well as at the
Plaza Hotel – so consider
these delicacies Michelin
star–worthy.

3.

4.

4.

3.

3.

4.

Brooklyn Heights & Dumbo   221

5.

VINEGAR HILL HOUSE
72 Hudson Ave, Dumbo
718 522 1018
www.vinegarhillhouse.com
Open Mon–Thurs 6–11pm,
Fri 6–11.30pm, Sat 10.30am–
3.30pm & 6–11.30pm,
Sun 10.30am–3.30pm

About five blocks from Dumbo
is the micro-neighbourhood of
Vinegar Hill – a cosy enclave
just three blocks wide and
two blocks long – made up
of cobblestoned streets and
19th century navy housing.
Opened by partners Sam
Buffa and chef Jean Adamson,
Vinegar Hill House is the
area's jewel. It's a serene
spot for a romantic dinner
or weekend brunch, with
covetable garden seating in
the warmer months.

The menu is short but
thoughtful, including a
signature skillet-cooked
chicken for dinner, and
a fruit-laced sourdough
pancake – created from
a 60-year-old starter – for
brunch. For dessert, indulge
in the moist and intense
chocolate cake, made with
Guinness and topped with
cream-cheese icing.

LOCAL TIP
A more casual offshoot in Dumbo, **VHH Foods** (55 Water St) is an all-day cafe and restaurant serving sandwiches, seasonal meat and vegetables, and 'next wave' cold-brew coffees with flavour profiles that mimic cocktail ingredients.

6.

INTERSECTION OF HENRY ST AND ATLANTIC AVE

From a Marie Antoinette–themed speakeasy to an old-time saloon – an amazing range of bars surround the corner of Henry Street and Atlantic Avenue

Floyd (131 Atlantic Ave) is folksy, relaxed fun. The menu is limited mostly to Kentucky beer cheese, beers and bourbons, but you're welcome to BYO food from the many nearby restaurants. There are sofas to lounge in, a jukebox, and – most surprisingly – a clay bocce court. The decor is modelled on taverns from the owner's hometown of Floyd, Iowa.

The landmark **Long Island Bar** (110 Atlantic Ave) was brought back to life in 2014, with its gorgeous mid-century interior and neon sign preserved. A classic cocktail menu by Cosmo-creator Toby Cecchini, along with red leather booths, Formica tables and a mirrored bar complete the scene. A substantial dinner menu is also on offer.

Chez Moi (135 Atlantic Ave) is a little touch of Paris. Lace-lined doors are opened to the street in the warm months, and the cocktail menu is a tribute to la belle France, with ingredients like absinthe, lavender and Lillet. There's even a signature bourbon cocktail topped with generous shavings of foie gras. Behind a false bookcase, stairs lead to a subterranean speakeasy, **Le Boudoir**, decked in red velvet in a tribute to Marie Antoinette's chambers in Versailles. Cocktails are served in ornate silver coupes, and bar snacks include crispy frogs' legs. There's live jazz on Mondays.

Elsa (136 Atlantic Ave) has a distinctly feminine aesthetic, from the whitewashed walls and fairy-lit courtyard to the fruit-forward cocktails, and bar-tap fashioned from a vintage sewing machine. Check out the bathroom lighting on their Instagram account, that makes every selfie poseur appear saintly.

Old-school cocktails are paired with grass-fed burgers and turkey-leg sandwiches at **Henry Public** (329 Henry St); an old-timey Brooklyn saloon, decorated with 1800s-era images, converted gas lights, bookshelves, a walnut bar and fireplace.

Montero Bar & Grill (73 Atlantic Ave) is the last of the dockworkers' bars on the Avenue, and stepping inside is a trip through time. Decorated with nautical paraphernalia and news clippings about the longshoremen and sailors who drank here, it's divey but good for a game of pool, an American beer, and a chat with an old timer.

Lined with benches, the half-kilometre-long **Brooklyn Heights Promenade** is a favourite place for lovers and friends to take in the view over to the Lower Manhattan skyline, the Statue of Liberty and Brooklyn Bridge – especially at sunset. The scenic walkway, also popular with joggers, is lined with grand mansions and brownstones and their well-tended gardens.

Brooklyn Bridge Park stretches two kilometres along the East River waterfront, from Atlantic Avenue in Cobble Hill all the way past the Manhattan Bridge in Dumbo, and includes six piers converted to sporting fields, basketball courts, playgrounds, a wildflower lawn, a roller rink and sand volleyball courts. Bike paths and pedestrian trails run throughout, and you can go kayaking or take in outdoor movies, all with breathtaking views of Lower Manhattan and New York Harbor.

Jane's Carousel can be accessed via entrances at Dock Street and Main Street. Built in 1922, the 48-horse carnival attraction was lovingly restored over a couple of decades by local artist Jane Walentas, then donated to Brooklyn Bridge Park. Closed year-round on Tuesday, and in winter only open Thursday to Sunday, it's housed in a beautiful transparent pavilion designed by Pritzker Prize–winning architect Jean Nouvel.

Appealing to the more adventurous theatregoer, **St Ann's Warehouse** (45 Water St) offers an avant-garde line-up of innovative music and stage. Past shows have included a production in the round of A Streetcar Named Desire, starring Gillian Anderson, and concerts by David Bowie, Rufus Wainwright and Laurie Anderson.

The most **popular Instagram spot** in Brooklyn is on cobblestoned Washington Street, between Front and Water streets, where you can capture a view of the Manhattan Bridge and the Empire State Building, perfectly framed by the historic red brick buildings of Dumbo.

When it opened in 1883, **Brooklyn Bridge** was deemed the Eighth Wonder of the World – a feat of engineering and beauty. You can walk or ride over it in either direction, but go from Brooklyn to Manhattan for superior views of the city skyline. A dedicated pedestrian lane and cycleway on the bridge's upper span is open 24 hours a day, and can be accessed from the intersection of Tillary Street and Boerum Place, or via an underpass on Washington Street (about two blocks from Front Street). Although it's only around 2 kilometres (1.25 miles) long, allow up to an hour for a leisurely stroll with stops for photos. Sunrise is a great time to avoid the crowds and see the sunrays bounce off the buildings. At the Manhattan end, a series of plaques detail the history of the bridge's construction.

The **Brooklyn Historical Society** (128 Pierrepont St) is a museum, library, educational centre and gift shop, dedicated to the study and preservation of Brooklyn's 400-year history. The building alone is extraordinary – an 1881 Queen Anne style of terracotta decoration, adorned with busts of Michelangelo, Beethoven, a Viking and a Native American, among others.

Berl's Brooklyn Poetry Shop (141 Front St) is the only store in the entire city dedicated solely to poetry.

These simpatico neighbourhoods, cheerfully grouped together as BoCoCa, feature beautiful brownstone architecture, independent boutiques, well-established butchers and bakeries, and a host of great restaurants and bars. You'll feel like a local strolling these streets.

While much of the food and fashion offerings are concentrated on Smith and Court Streets – there's also a hub of Italian–American food stores in Carroll Gardens, especially running east from Cou Street to Henry Street, including several bakeries (see p. 239) that have been trading continuously since the early 1900s.

Bergen St; Carroll St

*Different station locations for different subway lines

Buttermilk Channel

DEGRAW ST
STREET
SACKETT STREET
UNION STREET
VAN BRUNT
PRESIDENT STREET
STREET
CARROLL STREET
HUGH L. CAREY TUNNEL
BROOKLYN-BATTERY TUNNEL
Harold Ickes Playground
HAMILTON AVENUE
COLUMBIA
STREET
IMLAY
VAN BRUNT STREET
BOWNE STREET

24   JUN 8576

JHOP
1 EXIT 9 GIFT EMPORIUM
2 BIRD
3 REFINERY
4 BLACK GOLD RECORDS

EAT
5 BROOKLYN FARMACY AND SODA FOUNTAIN
6 LA VARA
7 BUTTERMILK CHANNEL
DRINK
8 JUNE

BOERUM HILL, COBBLE HILL & CARROLL GARDEN*J*

CONGRESS STREET

Cobble Hill Park

Nu Hotel

PACIFIC STREET

DEAN STREET

LinkNYC

BERGEN

LA VARA

WARREN STREET

BALTIC STREET

EXIT 9 GIFT EMPORIUM

BROOKLYN-QUEENS EXPRESSWAY

HICKS STREET

KANE STREET

STREET

STREET

WYCKOFF STREET

BOERUM HILL

BERGEN STREET

F G

COBBLE HILL

HENRY STREET

CLINTON STREET

TOMPKINS PLACE

STREET

LinkNYC

WARREN STREET

JUNE

LinkNYC

STREET

STREET

BROOKLYN FARMACY AND SODA FOUNTAIN

LinkNYC

Cobble Hill Cinemas

BALTIC STREET

LinkNYC

Boerum Park

COURT STREET

BUTLER STREET

BIRD

LinkNYC

STREET

HOYT STREET

DEGRAW STREET

COURT PASTRY SHOP

DOUGLASS STREET

BOOKS ARE MAGIC

SACKETT

UNION STREET

LinkNYC

REFINERY

STREET

MAZZOLA BAKERY

LinkNYC

LinkNYC

BATTERSBY

PRESIDENT STREET

CARROLL STREET

STREET

SACKETT

DEGRAW

STREET

SMITH STREET

STREET

F MONTELEONE BAKERY & CAFÉ

UNION STREET

STREET

Carroll Park

CARROLL GARDENS

NYC Parks

CARROLL STREET

F G

STREET

CLINTON STREET

2ND PLACE

1ST PLACE

PRESIDENT STREET

3RD

MILK BAR

BROOKLYN

STREET

CARROLL STREET

PLACE

PLACE

4TH PLACE

CAPUTO'S BAKE SHOP

3RD STREET

1ST STREET

2ND STREET

BLACK GOLD RECORDS

4TH

GOWANUS

LUQUER

COURT STREET

PRIME MEATS

ST

HOYT STREET

STREET

BOND STREET

Canal

N

0   100 m

BUTTERMILK CHANNEL

Gowanus

1.

EXIT 9 GIFT EMPORIUM

127 Smith St, Boerum Hill
718 422 7720
www.shopexit9.com
Open Mon–Fri 11am–7.30pm,
Sat 11am–8pm, Sun 12–7pm

Fancy a set of toy soldiers in yoga poses, or a Billie Holiday votive candle? How about a space-ready ice-cream sandwich, developed by NASA? This fun gift store is where you'll find all of the above, as well as David Bowie colouring books, solar-powered rainbow makers, and candles scented like fir trees. For an edgy piece of New York ephemera to gift or keep, you can't go past the curated range of locally made and city-centric merchandise, from tea towels and temporary tattoos to an illustrated book of New York etiquette. Lots of the goods are tongue-in-cheek, with Donald Trump dog poop bags on sale, a book of feminist icon cross-stitch patterns, and an action figure of Senator Elizabeth ('Nevertheless she persisted') Warren.

bird

BIRD

220 Smith St, Cobble Hill
718 797 3774
www.birdbrooklyn.com
Open Mon–Fri 12–8pm,
Sat–Sun 11am–7pm

Bird owner Jen Mankins describes herself as a 'failed minimalist', which is a reflection on the joyous patterned and embellished clothes she stocks, rather than on her sleek, architect-designed stores. All the wallflower-averse offerings – clothing, footwear, hats, bags and jewellery – are handpicked from around 150 emerging and established designers, including the colourful manga-bohemian Tsumori Chisato, and high-end folk aesthetics of Ulla Johnson and Isabel Marant. Expect to find lots of examples of homegrown talent, too, like Ace and Jig or Rachel Comey, as well as a thoughtful range of beauty products, including nail polishes handcrafted by L.A. jeweller Jess Hannah, and organic skincare products from eco-friendly Australian brand Grown Alchemist. The Cobble Hill shop is one of four Bird stores Mankins has established in Brooklyn since 1999 – with a flagship store in Williamsburg (which also sells menswear) and other outposts in Park Slope and Fort Greene.

LOCAL TIP
Bird aficionado and novelist Emma Straub owns **Books Are Magic** (225 Smith St), directly across the street, which hosts a great calendar of in-store author events.

3.

REFINERY
248 Smith St, Carroll Gardens
718 643 7861
Open Wed–Sat 12–7pm,
Sun 11.30am–6.30pm

Suzanne Bagdade has been trading to a steadfast clientele since the late 1990s, when she began selling her collection of handmade purses, totes and messenger bags, sewn in her Red Hook studio from vintage fabrics and leather. Also for sale at this Brooklyn staple are customisable Sven clogs from Sweden; colourful cotton scarves and knitted throws crafted by Indian artisans; African wax-print cotton blouses; mid-century crockery; felt necklaces and those cult classics of American footwear, Salt Water sandals.

LOCAL TIP
Across the road, **Battersby** (255 Smith St) is a sliver of a restaurant with a great reputation, serving a five-course tasting menu five nights a week.

BLACK GOLD RECORDS

461 Court St, Carroll Gardens
347 227 8227
www.blackgoldbrooklyn.com
Open Mon–Fri 7am–8pm,
Sat 8am–9pm, Sun 8am–7pm

This is one of those beautiful hybrid stores that Brooklyn does best. The record-cum-coffee shop also sells antiques – a lot of taxidermy and quirky vintage signage, as well as an eclectic range of macabre oil paintings, Ouija boards, anatomical prints, pulp sci-fi, and Americana. A couple of stools at the window and a bench outside mean you can settle in with your coffee – a velvety, dark quadruple-origin, customised for the store by a local roaster – and baked goods from Greenpoint's Ovenly. Allow plenty of time to browse the eclectic and hard-to-find vinyl collection and test it out at the listening station. Co-owner Jeff Ogiba updates the selection at least weekly. Expect to find psychedelic rock, obscure soul, funk and jazz, as well as 'whatever' – from horror movie soundtracks to limited colour-vinyl classics.

5.
BROOKLYN FARMACY AND SODA FOUNTAIN

513 Henry St, Carroll Gardens
718 522 6260
www.brooklynfarmacy
andsodafountain.com
Open Mon–Thurs 8.30am–
10pm, Fri 8.30am–11pm,
Sat 10am–11pm, Sun
10am–10pm

This place is a trip back to a more innocent time, with kids dropping by for a sundae after school, and couples sharing egg creams at the counter. Brother and sister Peter Freeman and Gia Giasullo resuscitated this beautiful 1920s apothecary, keeping its original cabinetry, penny-tile flooring and pressed-metal ceiling, and converting it to a modern soda fountain. Take your pick from 18 different kinds of sundaes, as well as milkshakes, ice-cream sandwiches, and the classic New York 'egg cream' – a concoction of milk, syrup and sparkling water, invented around 1900 and an old-world Brooklyn mainstay. Generous slices of in-season fruit pies are served from the counter top, as well as to-die-for chocolate chip cookies fresh from the oven.

6.
LA VARA

268 Clinton St, Cobble Hill
718 422 0065
www.lavarany.com
Open Mon–Thurs 5.30–10pm,
Fri 5.30–11pm, Sat 11.30am–
3.30pm & 5.30–11pm,
Sun 11.30am–3.30pm &
5.30–10pm

On a charming, tree-lined residential street sits La Vara – a tapas restaurant run by husband-and-wife Eder Montero and Alex Raij, who are credited with kick-starting the tapas craze in Chelsea in 2004 when they opened the acclaimed Tía Pol. Since they brought their exceptional 'cocina casera' (home cooking) over the East River in 2012, La Vara has been a hit since day one. Flavours explore Moorish and Jewish influences on northern Spanish cuisine. The crisp croqueta of the day is highly recommended, and there is plenty to satisfy the more courageous palate (grilled chicken hearts, stuffed rabbit loin, suckling pig). Try also the fideuà – a paella-style seafood dish from Valencia, made with noodles rather than rice, and the fried artichokes with anchovy aioli. Reservations are recommended for this chic and intimate space.

LOCAL TIP

Pop into **Milk Bar Bakery** (360 Smith St, Carroll Gardens) to sample cookies and innovative desserts by Momofuku pastry-chef Christina Tosi – including a slice of 'crack pie' (oat cookie crust and creamy filling) blended into cereal-milk soft serve.

7.

BUTTERMILK CHANNEL

524 Court St, Carroll Gardens
718 852 8490
www.buttermilkchannelnyc.com
Open Mon–Thurs 11.30am–
3pm & 5–10pm, Fri 11.30am–
3pm & 5–11.30pm, Sat
10am–3pm & 5–11.30pm,
Sun 10am–3pm & 5–10pm

Plan ahead for a visit to this casual whitewashed bistro – not just because it's extremely popular but because you'll need to leave room for the generous portions of American comfort food. It's known for its buttermilk fried chicken served with cheddar waffles, and its duck meatloaf, but pretty much everything is made with an unapologetic dose of hedonism. Mashed potatoes are whipped with buttermilk, the cornbread comes with maple butter, and even a simple grilled cheese sandwich offered on the Monday-to-Friday lunch menu is enhanced with double-smoked bacon. Book on a Monday night for a $40 three-course meal, or indulge your tippling side with corkage-free Tuesdays. The atmosphere is relaxed and friendly, with a large communal table taking up much of the dining room.

LOCAL TIP

A brilliant brunch or dinner from local ingredients can be found in nearby Alpine-inspired, carnivore-friendly brasserie **Prime Meats** (465 Court St, Carroll Gardens).

JUNE

231 Court St, Cobble Hill
917 909 0434
www.junebk.com
Open Mon–Thurs 5pm–12am,
Fri 5pm–1am, Sat 11am–4pm &
5.30pm–1am, Sun 11am–4pm
and 5.30pm–12am (happy hour
Mon–Fri 5–7pm)

The all-natural wine list is the point of difference at this beautiful spot, that evokes fin-de-siecle Paris with its curved leadlight panels and long marble bar, managing to be both elegant and cosy. Co-owner and chef Tom Kearney, from south Brooklyn farm-to-table restaurant **The Farm on Adderley**, brings the same ethos to the small plates offered at June, designed around seasonal vegetables combined perfectly with classic charcuterie. The dedication to thoughtful food production complements the bar's biodynamic and organic wines, which include plenty of affordable options. Weighted towards French and Italian producers, the diverse list also includes wine from Moravia, Spain, Germany, Austria, Australia and South Africa, as well as California and New York, and includes more than a dozen on-trend orange wines. If the weather is nice, grab a seat on the back patio.

On the block of Atlantic Avenue between Court and Henry streets, a cluster of Middle Eastern food stores offers a crash course in cuisines and a wonderful opportunity to pack a picnic. The Syrian proprietors of **Oriental Pastry & Grocery** (170 Atlantic Ave) specialise in sweets, including kounafa, a mouth-watering syrupy cheesecake and pistachio Turkish delight. Next door are a couple of Yemeni restaurants – the no-frills **Hadramout** (172 Atlantic Ave) and the stalwart **Yemen Café** (176 Atlantic Ave), which has been drawing food-curious customers since the 1980s to sample their bread and stews cooked in clay. Across the road, another longstanding purveyor, **Sahadi's** (187 Atlantic Ave), occupies three street-frontages, selling a vast range of Middle Eastern dried goods, olives and spices, an entire room of cheeses with experts to hand, as well as prepared foods, like dips and falafel, and a whole case of spanakopita and other pies. **Damascus Bread & Pastry Shop** (195 Atlantic Ave) is an old-school Syrian bakery, with flat bread so fresh you will want to eat it without accompaniments, satisfying savoury pies in whole wheat pastry, as well as glass-fronted counters piled with freshly made baklava. The chilled out **Mocha Hookah** (183 Atlantic Ave) is open 24 hours, where you can take your time over dip-and-vegetable platters, the generous range of fruit-flavoured tobaccos, and sweet Yemeni tea spiced with cardamom and cloves

From the early 1900s until the 1960s, Carroll Gardens became home to thousands of Italian migrant dock workers and their families. Their legacy lives on in the neighbourhood's concentration of specialty and family-owned bakeries. **Court Pastry Shop** (298 Court St), owned by the Zerilli family since 1948 and plastered with old family photos and newspaper clippings, is renowned for its sfogliatelle or 'lobster tails' (shell-shaped flaky pastry, filled with cream) as well as Italian ices served straight from a window to the street in the summer. Take the opportunity to eat in at **F Monteleone Bakery & Café** (355 Court St), in the same location since 1929 and specialising in Sicilian cookies, cannoli and colourful fondant-iced cakes, served cool from the fridge. At **Caputo's Bake Shop** (460 Court St), the specialty is bread and fresh mozzarella; made according to recipes brought over from Sicily over a century ago. A few blocks over, towards the East River, the quaint **Mazzola Bakery** (192 Union St), in this spot since 1928, takes special pride in its lard bread, homemade from a 90-year-old recipe using Genoa salami, provolone cheese, black pepper and lard. Nearby is classic Sicilian lunch spot, **Ferdinando's Focacceria** (151 Union St), opened in 1904 and still serving hard-to-find vastedda – a baked flat roll stuffed with calf spleen, ricotta and pecorino. Settle in, too, for the rice balls and the fluffy focaccia made with potato.

While you're in Carroll Gardens, take a stroll by the beautifully tended, 12-metre-deep (39.4 feet) front yards that give the neighbourhood its name. From First to Fourth Place, between Smith and Henry streets, many of the 19th century gardens also feature decorative fences and Madonna statuettes ('Mary on the half shell'), some life-sized.

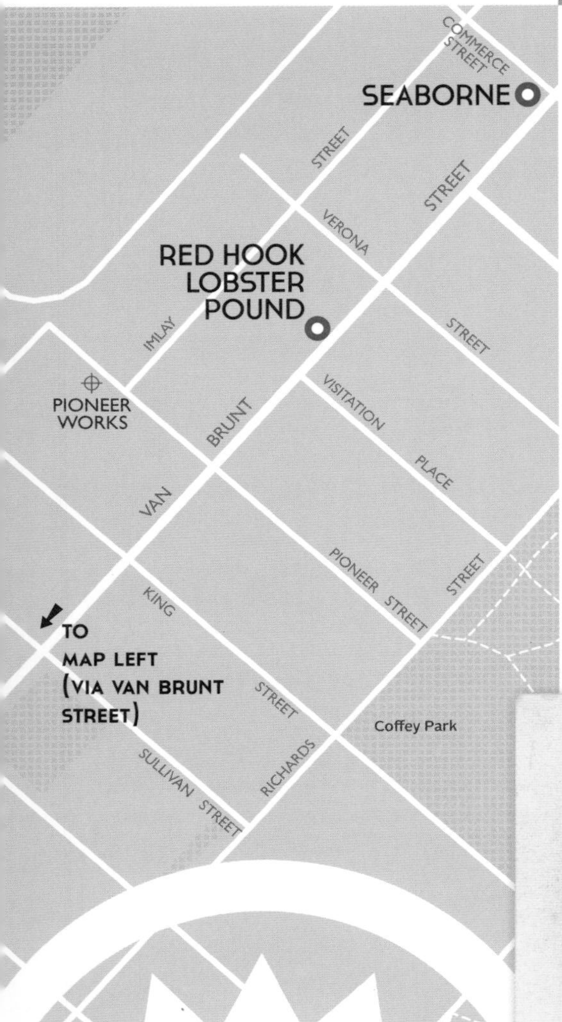

Bounded on three sides by water and without direct subway access, Red Hook has a seaside town feeling that is a welcome respite from New York's usual hectic pace. The formerly busy port is now home to a creative community – visual artists, artisanal distillers, bakers, chocolatiers, florists and winemakers.

Stroll down Van Brunt Street into boutiques, galleries, quirky bars and cafes that serve hearty farm-to-table fare. Arrive by ferry or water taxi from Lower Manhattan – there are great views of the Statue of Liberty.

🚇 Smith–9th Sts

*Different station locations for different subway lines

Map

SEABORNE

COMMERCE STREET

RED HOOK LOBSTER POUND

VERONA STREET

STREET

IMLAY

PIONEER WORKS

BRUNT

VAN

VISITATION PLACE

STREET

PIONEER STREET

KING

TO
MAP LEFT
(VIA VAN BRUNT STREET)

STREET

Coffey Park

SULLIVAN STREET

RICHARDS

RED HOOK

SHOP
1 Erie Basin
2 Wooden Sleepers

EAT
3 The Good Fork
4 Red Hook Lobster Pound
5 Hometown Bar-B-Que
6 Fort Defiance

DRINK
7 Seaborne
8 Sunny's Bar

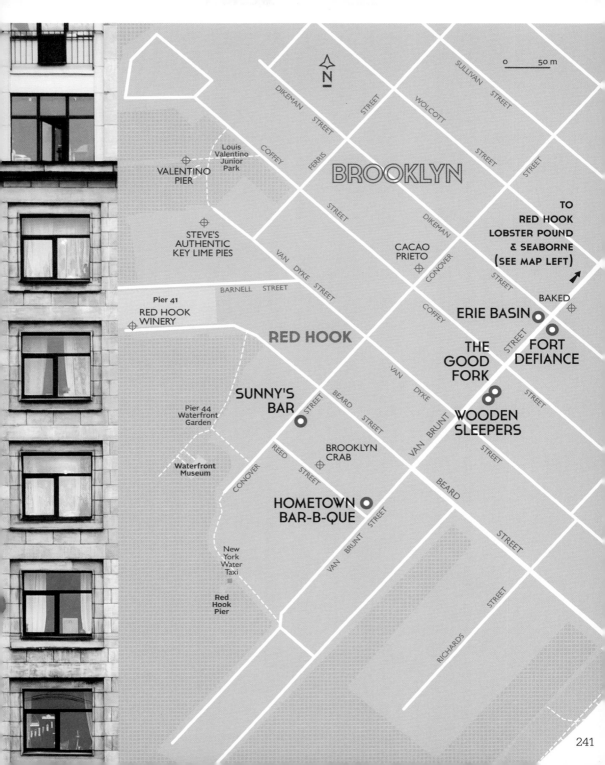

VALENTINO
PIER

Louis
Valentino
Junior
Park

COFFEY

DIKEMAN

STREET

FERRIS

STREET

WOLCOTT

SULLIVAN STREET

STREET

STREET

o   50 m

BROOKLYN

STEVE'S
AUTHENTIC
KEY LIME PIES

STREET

DIKEMAN

VAN DYKE STREET

CACAO
PRIETO

CONOVER

STREET

TO
RED HOOK
LOBSTER POUND
& SEABORNE
(SEE MAP LEFT)

BARNELL   STREET

Pier 41
RED HOOK
WINERY

COFFEY

BAKED

RED HOOK

VAN DYKE

ERIE BASIN

STREET

THE
GOOD
FORK

FORT
DEFIANCE

SUNNY'S
BAR

Pier 44
Waterfront
Garden

STREET

BEARD

STREET

VAN BRUNT

STREET

WOODEN
SLEEPERS

Waterfront
Museum

CONOVER

REED

STREET

BROOKLYN
CRAB

STREET

BEARD

HOMETOWN
BAR-B-QUE

VAN BRUNT STREET

STREET

STREET

New
York
Water
Taxi

RICHARDS

STREET

Red
Hook
Pier

ERIE BASIN

388 Van Brunt St
718 554 6147
www.eriebasin.com
Open Wed–Sat 12–6pm

This pioneering jewellery boutique is named for a nearby waterway. When it opened in 2006, it soon built a loyal following for its beautifully curated Victorian engagement rings and wedding bands. A decade later, the store is still staffed by gentle Midwesterner Russell Whitmore, whose art-trained eye is put to good use in all the buying.

In addition to the sought-after rings, you'll find an eclectic range – 1920s Egyptian-revival brooches, Chinese cloisonné fish pendants with secret compartments, sculptural mid-century Scandinavian pieces – with an emphasis on vintage items 'that still look modern'.

Since 2014, Whitmore has also been designing a locally made line of fine jewellery, called EB, that is sleek and contemporary but inspired by antique motifs.

2.

WOODEN SLEEPERS
395 Van Brunt St
718 643 0802
www.wooden-sleepers.com
Open Wed–Sun 11am–7pm,
Mon–Tues by appointment

Brian Davis' attraction to Red Hook comes from his upbringing in a small waterfront town on the far end of Long Island. It's an effect he has reproduced in his cabin-like vintage menswear store. The look is 'classic American Northeast Atlantic', he says of his smartly edited collection of vintage workwear, sportswear, and military and collegiate clothing, made between the 1920s and 1990s. Expect to find vintage khakis, nicely worn-in t-shirts, 1950s tweed jackets, and plaid and chambray shirts at similar prices to chain stores but every item unique. Davis favours authentic design and timeless style.

The store also offers a selection of books, blankets and other hand-picked items of manly ephemera.

3.
THE GOOD FORK
391 Van Brunt St
718 643 6636
www.goodfork.com
Open Tues–Fri 5.30–10.30pm,
Sat 10am–3pm & 5.30–
10.30pm, Sun 10am–3pm &
5.30–10pm

The decor in this restaurant is as unusual and pleasing as the food. Handcrafted by cabinetmaker and co-owner Ben Schneider, the warmly lit dining room – deep and narrow with curved wooden ceilings – feels like the interior of a fine sailing ship, far out to sea. Along with feeling appealingly secluded, it's a lovely nod to the neighbourhood's maritime history.

Chef Sohui Kim, Schneider's wife, delivers the culinary artistry, serving up beautifully executed comfort food with a Korean inflection. Roasted free-range chicken is accompanied by a fermented black bean butter sauce, while her burger is spiced up with kimchi. Her fusion touches are also found in the eclectic brunch offerings that include delicious bibimbap (a warm dish of rice with sautéed vegetables, prime steak and fried egg, with tangy Korean red-chilli sauce), pork dumplings, and sesame granola, alongside more conventional bacon and eggs.

4.
RED HOOK LOBSTER POUND
284 Van Brunt St
718 858 7650
www.redhooklobster.com/pound
Open Tues–Thurs 11.30am–10pm, Fri–Sat 11.30am–11pm, Sun 11.30am–10pm

----

Lobster may be associated with luxury cuisine, but in this affordable, no-fuss diner-cum-sports bar it's all about the freshest Maine crustaceans served up in soft white rolls, tucked into macaroni and cheese, or piled onto cheese fries. Although summers spent in Maine provided their inspiration, proprietors Ralph Gorman and Susan Povich are lobster-roll agnostics these days, offering both Connecticut (warm with butter and lemon) and Maine (cold with homemade mayo) varieties.

In keeping with the restaurant's beachside decor of nautical flags and picnic-style seating, the bathroom notably goes all out with fun-house mirrors and a soundtrack of crashing waves and seagulls.

3.

4.

LOCAL TIP
Head a few blocks south to the multi-level **Brooklyn Crab** (24 Reed St) for water views from the upper deck, and mini-golf and beanbag toss games near the ground-floor bar.

5.

HOMETOWN BAR-B-QUE

454 Van Brunt St
347 294 4644
www.hometownbarbque.com
Open Tues–Thurs 12–11pm,
Fri–Sat 12pm–12am,
Sun 12–11pm

There's something appealingly primal about a Southern barbecue – the rich aromas, the generous quantities of tender meat piled without ceremony onto metal trays, the just-as-filling 'sides' of potato salad, mac and cheese, collard greens and cornbread. Hometown's pitmaster Billy Durney has made a specialty of smoking the meats on oak wood, then adding flavours that give a nod to Brooklyn's diversity – from Caribbean jerk ribs to fried Korean sticky ribs.

It's not just the servings that are oversized here – the restaurant is housed in a huge converted garage, with an enormous American flag painted on one wall. Highly recommended is Durney's beef rib, which is cooked overnight for 15 hours.

Although the wait in line for food can be lengthy, there's no question your appetite will be satisfied.

6.

FORT DEFIANCE

365 Van Brunt St
347 453 6672
www.fortdefiancebrooklyn.com
Open Mon & Wed–Fri
10–12am, Tues 10am–3pm,
Sat–Sun 9–12am

Straightforward American fare that allows locally sourced ingredients to shine is the aim at this buzzy all-day hub. But owner St. John Frizell is also a bartender and drink writer, hence the excellent cocktails that are good enough to attract drinkers from well beyond the local area, and the inspiration for the generous bar seating. Every Thursday night this homey bar-cafe also transforms into a lively tiki bar, the Sunken Harbor Club, with a themed menu.

If you're exploring the neighbourhood on a weekend, this is a great brunch spot and on a sunny day you could get lucky and nab one of the outside stools that line the large windows open to the street. For a very Southern brunch, order the Charleston (poached eggs with collard greens, cornbread and a mustard hollandaise), with the classic New Orleans brunch cocktail, the Ramos gin fizz. The frothy concoction of gin, orange blossom water, cream and egg white is shaken for several minutes, testing any bartender's mettle.

LOCAL TIP

Nip across Dikeman Street to **Baked** (359 Van Brunt St) to try its original creation, the Brookster – a brownie tart base filled with choc chunk cookie batter.

5.

6.

6.

7.

SEABORNE
228 Van Brunt St
718 852 4888
Open Thurs–Sun 5pm–3am

If you fancy pairing tailor-made cocktails with pinball games, you're in luck at this secluded hole-in-the-wall venue. Designed to be staffed by a single bartender, it has quirky decor that resembles a tiny diner. Leather booths are fitted with individual spigots for water refills, and a box of playing cards sits on each table. In keeping with the down-low vibe, a back room holds several pinball machines – a pastime that was banned in New York City until the 1970s, and heavily punished by the police if discovered.

Originally the vision of New York's late master mixologist, Sasha Petraske (Milk & Honey and **Little Branch**, *see* p. 078), Seaborne has a classic cocktail menu, but you're encouraged to opt for the 'bartender's choice' – concocted from your favourite ingredients. The rules of barroom etiquette are the same as those Petraske posted in his celebrated (now-shuttered) speakeasy Milk & Honey, including 'Gentlemen will not introduce themselves to ladies' and 'No hooting, hollering, shouting or other loud behaviour'.

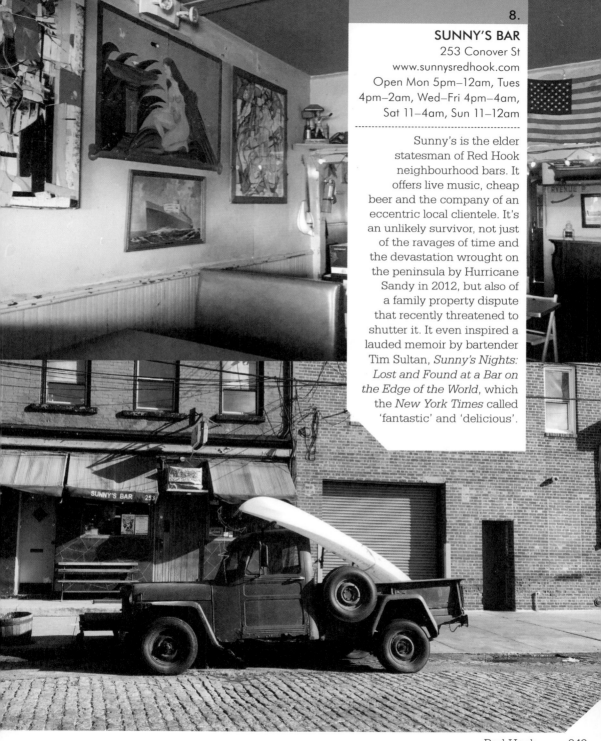

SUNNY'S BAR
253 Conover St
www.sunnysredhook.com
Open Mon 5pm–12am, Tues
4pm–2am, Wed–Fri 4pm–4am,
Sat 11–4am, Sun 11–12am

Sunny's is the elder statesman of Red Hook neighbourhood bars. It offers live music, cheap beer and the company of an eccentric local clientele. It's an unlikely survivor, not just of the ravages of time and the devastation wrought on the peninsula by Hurricane Sandy in 2012, but also of a family property dispute that recently threatened to shutter it. It even inspired a lauded memoir by bartender Tim Sultan, *Sunny's Nights: Lost and Found at a Bar on the Edge of the World*, which the *New York Times* called 'fantastic' and 'delicious'.

Red Hook is home to a hive of small industries, from art studios to distilleries. Just off Van Brunt Street is **Cacao Prieto** (218 Conover St), where single-origin organic beans and sugar imported from the Dominican Republic are transformed daily into chocolate, bon-bons and small-batch cacao-based liqueurs and rums. Take a tour of the factory and distillery on weekends, with tasting flights of chocolate and spirits included.

A few blocks over, you can also get a look behind the scenes at the **Van Brunt Stillhouse** (6 Bay St) and indulge in a tasting of its made-from-scratch whiskies, which use grains sourced from upstate farmers – straight, on the rocks or in a cocktail. More recently, the distillery collaborated with neighbourhood winemakers to produce a small-batch grappa. **Red Hook Winery** (175 Van Dyke St) makes wines using only New York–grown grapes, and offers daily tastings.

When planning your visit to Red Hook, check out the program at **Pioneer Works** (159 Pioneer St) – an eclectic offering of exhibitions, performances and events in an enormous brick warehouse that used to house an ironworks. Developed by local artist Dustin Yellin, the property also includes a quirky landscaped garden, dotted with artworks. On-site store **Pioneer Books** sells a mix of titles that reflect the cultural institution's eclectic programming.

Although the view is lovely at all times of the day, **Valentino Pier** (at Ferris St) is a magnet for romantics hoping to catch a beautiful sunset.

Grab one of **Steve's Authentic Key Lime Pies** (185 Van Dyke St) and enjoy the free films that screen at the pier in the summer. The pier is also the best location in New York City to capture a fully frontal view of the Statue of Liberty, which is oriented to face France, the country that gifted the statue in 1885.

Five minutes away around the shoreline, and sharing the same knockout views of the 46-metre (151-foot) statue, is the little **Waterfront Museum** (290 Conover St), housed aboard a century-old barge. The Lehigh Valley Barge #79, built in 1914, is open to visitors on Thursday and Saturday afternoons, and also hosts a program of performances and art exhibits year-round. Museum founder, local character and former cruise-ship juggler 'Captain' David Sharps, who lives on board, has a wealth of stories about the history of the Brooklyn waterfront. Be sure to ask him to activate the fascinating George Rhoads audio-kinetic 'ball machine' sculpture.

Here are just some of the many attractions, well worth exploring, in New York's other major boroughs.

QUEENS

New York's largest borough boasts sporting events and a thriving seaside scene, some of the city's best ethnic cuisine and fascinating museums.

Queens Museum (Flushing Meadows, Corona Park), built for the 1939 World's Fair, holds a collection of gorgeous retro memorabilia from this event and the 1964 Fair, including its most famous permanent installation – an 867-square-metre (9332 square foot) miniature Panorama of the City of New York, created by more than 100 people over three years.

Film, TV and digital media enthusiasts should visit **The Museum of the Moving Image** (36-01 35th Ave, Astoria), with its permanent display of over 1400 artefacts, from 19th century optical toys to video games, plus wonderful temporary exhibitions, screenings and installations.

Innovative and experimental, **MoMA PS1** (22-25 Jackson Ave, Long Island City) is dedicated to contemporary art, and home to the ultra-hip Warm Up summer music series that attracts a stellar line-up of bands and DJs. In colder months, the Sunday Sessions performance series showcases music, dance, conversations and film.

Queens is New York's most ethnically diverse neighbourhood with a vibrant food scene – most notably the Greek eateries of Astoria and the Chinese and Korean food in Flushing. Also noteworthy is **Arepa Lady** in Jackson Heights (78–31 37th Ave), serving arepas (griddled corn cakes with kneaded-in mozzarella, served with a range of meats), patacones and chuzos, since first opening as a food cart under the train line back in 1990.

Queens' burgeoning micro-brewing scene offers tap rooms and tours. **Single Cut Beersmiths** (19–33 37th St, Astoria) make hop-driven beers that can be sampled from their smokehouse. **Transmitter Brewing** (53–02 11th St, Long Island City) focuses on traditional and farmhouse ales.

Big Alice Brewing (8-08 43rd Rd, Long Island City) is known for its highly creative small batches, while **Rockaway Brewing Company** (46–01 5th St, Long Island City) plays reggae at tastings and includes notes of papaya, pineapple and hibiscus in brews. **Finback Brewery** (7801 77th St, Woodhaven) favours engineered hop-forward, sour and dark beers, with enigmatic names like Smoke Detection.

Brooklyn Grange (37–18 Northern Blvd, Long Island City) runs the world's largest rooftop soil farm, growing almost 23 tonnes of organic food a year and keeping honey bees. Visit from May to October to buy produce, take a farm tour or participate in an amazing Sunday afternoon **Butcher Paper Dinner** created by some of the city's most innovative chefs, and served at a 15-metre table with a spectacular view of the Manhattan skyline. Sign up for their newsletter as events usually sell out within 24 hours.

Flushing Meadows-Corona Park, the city's second biggest park after Central Park, is home to the **Queens Botanical Garden** (43–50 Main St, Flushing).

New York Hall of Science (47–01 111th St, Corona) houses a 3D theatre and a huge interactive space simulating jungle, desert and mountain valley environments.

Citi Field is the home ground of the **Mets** baseball team, whose season runs from April to October (Roosevelt Ave at 126th St, Corona) and the **National Tennis Center** is where the **U.S. Open** is held at the end of summer.

Created by artists and activists in 1986, the 1.8 hectare **Socrates Sculpture Park** (32-01 Vernon Blvd, Long Island City) has exhibits, a greenmarket, yoga, tai chi, kayaking, and a gorgeous view over the city skyline.

For a day at the beach, catch the A subway train or the ferry to **Rockaway**. As well as surfing, swimming and the 8-kilometre Boardwalk, there's a thriving street food scene, with heavy emphasis on Latin cuisine – from Mexico, Brazil, Colombia and Venezuela.

THE BRONX

Head to New York's northernmost borough for outdoor cultural and sporting attractions.

What could be more quintessentially New York than a trip to **Yankee Stadium** (1 East 161st St) to see one of the most successful teams in baseball history play at their home ground? When they win, Sinatra's 'New York, New York' blares over the speaker system – a heart-warmingly timeless tradition.

Founded in 1891, the **New York Botanical Garden** (2900 Southern Blvd) is an expansive wonderland of more than a million plants on 100 hectares (247 acres). Wander through old-growth forest, a rose garden, Japanese garden, wetlands, and a huge Crystal Palace–style greenhouse, built in the 1890s. Recent seasonal exhibits include 20 massive coloured glass installations by artist Dale Chihuly, and a re-creation of Frida Kahlo and Diego Rivera's gardens at their Mexico City home.

Home to more than 6000 animals, all in naturalistic settings – from the Congo Gorilla Forest to the snow leopards of the Himalayan Highlands – the world-famous **Bronx Zoo** (2300 Southern Blvd) is the largest city zoo in the United States. It now boasts a 120-metre (393.7 foot) zip line that was installed in 2017, letting visitors sail 15-metres (49.2 feet) above the treetops and Bronx River, plus a nature trek and seven aerial rope courses, including one for extreme sports enthusiasts, with a huge jump at the end.

The vast 19th century **Woodlawn Cemetery** (Jerome Ave at Bainbridge Ave) features artist-and-architect-designed monuments and mausoleums, and is the final resting place for more than 300,000 people, including prominent New Yorkers – jazz musicians Miles Davis and Duke Ellington, author Herman Melville, and suffragist Elizabeth Cady Stanton. Guided tours are run by The Woodlawn Conservancy (www.woodlawnconservancy.org).

Connected by bridge to the mainland of the Bronx is the seafood utopia of **City Island** – as close as you'll get to visiting a quaint New England coastal town without leaving the city. Just 2.5 kilometres (1.5 miles) long and less than a kilometre (0.6 miles) wide, it offers several eateries to choose from along City Island Avenue (some cash only), including **The Original Crab Shanty Restaurant**, housed in an old silent movie theatre, or take a quick left off the bridge as you arrive, to dine at **City Island Lobster House** (691 Bridge St, City Island).

SOUTH BROOKLYN

As an entertainment precinct, **Coney Island** (1208 Surf Ave) goes into hibernation during the winter. During the warm months, however, this zany southernmost outpost of Brooklyn is a law unto itself, and well worth a nostalgic visit to take in the quaint attractions of **Deno's Wonder Wheel Amusement Park** (3059 W 12th St) and the wooden Cyclone roller coaster at **Luna Park** (1000 Surf Ave); **Nathan's Famous** hot dogs (1310 Surf Ave) and the **New York Aquarium** (602 Surf Ave). Each year in June, the streets are taken over by the outlandish **Mermaid Day Parade** (many spectators dress up, too). Catch the D, F, N or Q subway to the end of the line at Stillwell Ave, between May and September, to participate in the neighbourhood's high season.

Neighbouring **Brighton Beach** (sometimes referred to as 'Little Odessa' for its significant Ukrainian community) has most signage in Cyrillic as well as English, and an eclectic array of food, gift, and fur stores, plus bars, clubs and restaurants with a distinctly Eastern European flavour. Take a walk on the Boardwalk, browse the bookstores and dine on some xachapuri (Georgian flatbread filled with cheese), plov (Uzbek rice pilaf) or meaty Ukrainian borscht, preferably accompanied by some vodka.

The island of Manhattan is just one of five boroughs in the city – the others being Brooklyn, the Bronx, Queens and Staten Island. New York is big but it's easy to get around. See www.mta.info for more information.

ARRIVING BY AIR

New York is serviced by three airports:

John F. Kennedy International Airport (JFK) is New York's major international airport, in Queens, about 24 kilometres (15 miles) from Midtown Manhattan. It has six terminals, numbers 1–8 (3 and 6 were demolished). Travel free between terminals via the AirTrain (see right), or pay $5 if using it to connect to and from the city's subway train system.

LaGuardia Airport (LGA) is New York's second-largest airport, also located in Queens, about 13 kilometres (8 miles) from Midtown Manhattan, directly across the East River. A complimentary shuttle bus service runs between its four terminals.

Newark International Airport (EWR) has three terminals, connected by courtesy buses, and is in New Jersey – handier to the west side of Manhattan.

Airport taxis

Taxis from JFK to Manhattan take around 30–60 minutes, with a flat fare of $52.50, but fares to Brooklyn or elsewhere are metered.

From LaGuardia, taxis take around 25 minutes on a metered fare of $30–$40.

Metered taxi fares from Newark to Midtown Manhattan are about $50–$75, plus tolls and tip, and take around 45–60 minutes. During rush hour there's a $5 surcharge. Travelling back to Newark from the city via yellow taxi will attract a $17.50 surcharge, in addition to tolls and tip.

Airport buses

Two express buses serve LaGuardia: the M60 and Q70. The M60 runs to Harlem, and connects to all major subway lines in the city. The non-stop Q70 connects with a subway hub with five lines at Jackson Heights/Roosevelt Avenue. *See*: www.tripplanner.mta.info.

For shuttle bus information for all three airports, *see* www.nycairporter.com, www.goairlinkshuttle.com and www.supershuttle.com. For an additional Newark service, *see* www.newarkairportexpress.com

Airport trains

AirTrain (*see* www.panynj.gov/airports/jfk-airtrain) travels free between the terminals of JFK, and links the airport to the subway and **Long Island Rail Road** (LIRR) for a fare of $5. Connect to the A subway stop at Howard Beach/JFK Airport station, or the E, J or Z at Sutphin Blvd/JFK Airport. The subway takes an additional 60–75 minutes to reach Midtown Manhattan. The LIRR from Jamaica Station in Queens to Penn Station in Manhattan takes around 20 minutes.

AirTrain links Newark to Midtown Manhattan via NJ Transit and Amtrak's EWR train station, for a trip of between 45–90 minutes. Keep your ticket after using it to exit the AirTrain station, as it is also used for the NJ Transit fare or Amtrak. The **PATH** (Port Authority Trans Hudson) provides rapid transit between several stops in New York City and New Jersey, including between Newark Liberty International Airport (from Penn Station – *not* the same as the one in Manhattan) and stops in lower and midtown Manhattan.

ARRIVING BY TRAIN

NYC has two main rail stations, both in Midtown:

Grand Central Terminal is on the east side, and is the main terminal for Metro–North Railroad, which goes to parts of upstate New York and Connecticut, as well as the 4, 5, 6, 7 and S (shuttle to Times Square) subway lines.

Penn Station is on the west side and is the terminal for the Long Island Rail Road (serving Long Island), Amtrak (connecting to many points throughout the US), and NJ Transit (serving New Jersey), as well as connecting to the 1, 2, 3, A, C and E subway lines.

GETTING AROUND

Walking tips

Manhattan is great for walking, as there is a lot of flat terrain and often the short distances between sights make it not worth catching the subway.

- Americans drive on the right, so look both ways before crossing.
- On the footpaths, walk on the right, overtake on the left and pull over to the side to consult your phone or admire a building.
- Take care on crossings, as vehicles don't automatically yield to pedestrians as they go around corners. Always look both ways on one-way streets and cross with care even when you have the right of way.

Tickets

Use a Metrocard on Metropolitan Transportation Authority (MTA) New York City Transit subways, local buses and express buses, as well as the JFK AirTrain, MTA Staten Island Railway, and the Roosevelt Island Tram. Metrocards can be purchased at subway stations from vending machines (cash, debit and credit cards) and staffed booths (cash only) and come in three kinds:

- A Single Ride Card, only available from vending machines, costs $3, doesn't allow transfers, and must be used within two hours of purchase.
- A Pay-Per-Ride Card allows commuters to put $5.50–$100 on a reusable card.
- An Unlimited Ride Card lasts for either seven days ($31) or 30 days ($116.50).
- Express bus rides cost $6.50.

Up to three children, with a maximum height each of 112 centimetres (44 inches), can ride on subways and buses free when travelling with a fare-paying adult.

Subway tips

- The easiest and quickest way to travel around New York City, open 24 hours a day, seven days a week.

- Pay attention to 'uptown' and 'downtown' station entrances, which can be across the street from one another, and to signs on the platform.
- You can get a free subway map from any booth attendant, or download one from www.mta.info
- Subway lines sometimes change routes or do not run late at night and on weekends, due to maintenance work. *See* www.tripplanner.mta. info for updated service information.

Subway safety

- Elevator access to the subway is limited.
- Have your Metrocard ready before you go through the turnstiles.
- On escalators, stand on the right, walk on the left.
- When the train pulls in, stand to each side of the doors to allow passengers to get off before entering.
- Give a seat to pregnant women, the elderly, disabled and children.
- Avoid empty carriages – usually there's been a smell or spill.
- Keep your belongings close, and avoid travelling alone late at night – crime is low but be alert.
- Only 19 per cent of the city's subway stations are fully accessible for people with disabilities. Find an up-to-date list of accessible stations at www.web.mta.info/accessibility/stations.htm.

Bus tips

Buses are more useful in boroughs other than Manhattan, where the subway and walking are more efficient modes of transport.

- Schedules and route maps are posted at bus stops.
- Most buses run every 5–15 minutes and many buses run 24 hours a day, seven days a week.
- With a smartphone, you can scan the QR code at the bus stop to find out when the next bus should arrive.
- Check on the front of the bus if it is making all or only limited stops. Buses generally stop

every block on cross-street routes, and every second block on avenue routes. Late at night, drivers will often pull up between stops for you on request, if they consider it is safe.

- A single fare will take you any distance along the route and all buses accept Metrocards or exact coin change.

Select Bus Service (SBS) routes have payment kiosks on the footpath next to the stop. Designed to improve transport flow on long, busy corridors, SBS buses have longer spaces between stops and payment kiosks to speed up travel.

Yellow taxi tips

- Taxis are available 24 hours a day but are difficult to secure when it rains, or between 4pm and 5pm when shifts change.
- When the centre numbers on top are illuminated it means taxis are on duty.
- By law, drivers can't refuse to take you any distance.
- Taxis accept cash, credit or debit card and expect a tip.
- There's a minimum metered fare of $2.50 and various surcharges between 4pm and 6am.

Green Boro Taxis can pick up passengers in outer boroughs (not including JFK and LaGuardia Airports) and in Manhattan above East 96th and West 110th streets. Green Boro passengers can be dropped anywhere, but don't attempt to hail a ride in the 'yellow zone' south of East 96th and West 110th streets.

Further information about taxi travel can be found on the **NYC Taxi and Limousine Commission** website, *see* www.nyc.gov/tlc.

Uber is an aggressive competitor in the taxi market in New York City, including a reduced-price pooling option, and operates in all the outer boroughs, where cabs can be scarcer.

Cycling tips

- Traffic can be hectic but the city is well served with bike lanes, and drivers are accustomed to sharing the road with cyclists.
- There are great bike paths in Central, Riverside and Prospect Parks, as well as along the Hudson and East rivers and on many of the bridges.
- Cyclists under the age of 14 are legally required to wear a helmet.

Ride the City (www.ridethecity.com) can recommend the safest route to get from A to B.

Get a downloadable bike map and a guide to cycling in the city at www.nyc.gov/bikemap.

Citi Bike (www.citibikenyc.com) makes thousands of bikes available at the 600 Citi Bike station kiosks across Manhattan, Brooklyn, Queens and Jersey City, 24 hours a day, seven days a week. Visitors can buy a short-term pass (a 24-hour pass for $12, or a 3-day pass for $72) through the Citi Bike app or at one of the station kiosks. A map and instructions can be found online.

Bus and walking tours

An incredible range of bus and walking tours are available. The city's excellent official guide site (*see* www.nycgo.com) has hundreds of options.

Ferries

NYC Ferry, *see* www.ferry.nyc, is a city-wide network, with East River docks at 34th Street and Wall Street, and multiple stops in Brooklyn and Queens, as well as Governors Island and Rockaway Beach. A ride costs $2.75 and tickets can be purchased from vending machines at landings, from ticket agents at Pier 11/Wall Street, or you can go paperless by using the NYC Ferry app. A $1 surcharge applies when you bring a bike.

The **Staten Island Ferry**, *see* www.siferry.com, is a free, 25-minute service, which takes in great views of the Statue of Liberty, New York Harbor and Lower Manhattan, departing from Whitehall Terminal (4 Whitehall St).

PUBLIC HOLIDAYS

New Year's Day (1 January)

Birthday of Martin Luther King, Jr (third Monday in January)

Washington's Birthday (third Monday in February)

Memorial Day (the last Monday in May)

Independence Day (4 July)

Labor Day (the first Monday in September)

Columbus Day (second Monday in October)

Veterans Day (11 November)

Thanksgiving (the fourth Thursday in November)

Christmas Day (25 December).

TIPPING AND TAX

Many goods and services attract a sales tax of 8.9 per cent, not indicated on the price tag. Exceptions include food purchased at the grocery store, and clothing and footwear under $110.

Tipping is expected in New York, and many service professionals' wages are based on being supplemented by tips. It's good to keep small bills in your wallet for this purpose.

Airport shuttle: No tip is necessary but $1 per bag is a courtesy if the driver assists you.

Bars: $1 per drink ($2 at upscale establishments).

Hotels: Bell hops $1–$2 per bag; hotel maids $2 per day of your stay; doorperson $1–$2 for hailing a cab; concierge $3–$5 for dinner reservations or tour arrangements, $10 for more unusual services, like getting your laptop repaired.

Restaurants: Many are beginning to implement no-tipping policies, instead listing a service charge on the menu or bill. Otherwise 15–20 per cent. Try to tip in cash to ensure the money goes to the server.

Spa attendants and hair stylists: 15–20 per cent.

Taxi drivers: 15–20 per cent. Try to tip in cash to ensure the money goes to the driver.

WI-FI

All 279 underground subway stations offer wi-fi: Select SSID TransitWirelessWiFi.

The city has introduced a free, super-fast wi-fi network LinkNYC (see www.link.nyc) that also provides device-charging stations.

Many cafes, museums and libraries offer free wi-fi.

TOURIST INFORMATION AND CONSULAR ASSISTANCE

There are three **Official NYC Information Centres** in Manhattan offering guides, maps, discounted passes and additional advice:

Macy's Herald Square: 151 West 34th St (between Seventh Ave and Broadway)

Times Square Plaza: Between Seventh Ave, Broadway, 44th St and 45th St

City Hall: Southern tip of City Hall Park on the Broadway footpath at Park Row

The **Brooklyn Tourism and Visitor Centre** (Brooklyn Borough Hall, 209 Joralemon St) in Downtown Brooklyn, supplies information, brochures and Brooklyn-made products.

Australian Consulate General
150 East 42nd St, Level 34
212 351 6500

British Consulate General
845 Third Ave
212 745 0200

Consulate General of Canada
1251 Avenue of the Americas, Concourse Level
212 596 1628

New Zealand Consulate General
295 Madison Ave, Level 41
212 832 4038

South African Consulate General
333 East 38th St
212 213 4880

INDEX

Photography credits

All photography © Pip Cummings except the following:
(Letters indicate where multiple images appear on a page, from top to bottom,
left to right)

Back cover: iStock Photo/Jaz Lazarin; Endpaper Nickel and Diner; i Jonah
Rosenberg; iv-v (f, p), ix, 161, 221 (a, c, e) Katie June Burton; 3 The Mysterious
Bookshop; 4 (a), 5 (a, c, f) Noah Fecks (b) Matthew Salacuse; 5 (b, d), 164 (b),
165 (b) Matthew Williams; 5 (e) Matthew Salacuse; 6 - 7 (a, c) Bubby's; iv-v (j),
6 (a), 7 (a, c) Bubby's; iv-v (j), 8-9 (a) Dead Rabbit Grocery and Grog; 9 (b) Paul
Wagtouicz; 14 (b) Jonah Rosenberg; iv-v (c, n), 14 (c) Michele Varian; 15 (c)
3x1; 16 (a) Noe DeWitt; 16 (b), 17 (a) Michael Grimm; 17 (b), 160, 244-245 (b)
Daniel Krieger; 18 (a), 19 (b) Thomas Schauer; 20 (a) Charles de Vaivre; 20 (b),
21 (a,e) Annie Schlecter; 21 (b, c, d, f) AvroKO Hospitality Group; 26, 27 (a)
Le Labo; 28, 63 Yvonne Brooks; 30 (a), 31 (c) Café Gitane; 30 (b), 31 (a, b), 33,
39, 40 (a), 41 (a, c), 44-45, 50 (a), 51, 54-55, 57 Tim Slade; 32 Marco Monti; 40
(b), 41 (b) Nicole Franzen; 42 Dimes; 43 Chinese Tuxedo; 52 Driely S; 53 Eric
Wolfinger; 62, 64 (a), 65 (b), 66 (b), 67 (b), 69 (c), 75, 114, 115 (b,c), 129, 134,
135, 182 (a,c), 183, 184, 188 (b), 189, 207 Bernard Watt; 64 (b), 65 (c) Minetta
Tavern; 65 (a), 80-81 Emilie Baltz; 66 (a) Michael Condran; iv-v (m), 67 (a) Miss
Lily's; 68 Blue Note Jazz Club; 69 (a, b) Comedy Cellar; 74 Aedes de Venustus;
76 (b), 77 (b, d, e, f) The Spotted Pig; 78 (a), 79 (a, b) The Elk; 78 (b), 79 (c) Little
Branch; 86 (a), 87 (c) Azikiwe Mohammed; 86 (b), 87 (a, b) Story; 88 (b), 89 (b,
d, f) Santina; 90 Empire Diner; 91 Zach DeZon; 92 Oleg March; 93 Standard
Hotels; 100 (a) Evan Joseph; 100 (b) Virginia Rollison; iv-v (i), 101 (a), 102 (a)
Liz Clayman; 101 (b) Shake Shack; 102 (b), 103 (b, f) Jade Young; 103 (a, c,
d), 105 (a) Daniel Krieger, Liz Clayman, Ellen Silverman; 103 (e) Ivan Halpern;
104 Raines Law Room; 105 (b) Nathan McCarley-O'Neill; 112 Josh Wong;
115 (a) Wafels & Dinges; 116 Grand Central Oyster Bar; 117 Bar SixtyFive at
Rainbow Room; 122 (a), 123 (b) Kitchen Arts and Letters; 122 (b); 123 (a,c)
Tender Buttons; 124 Hulya Kolabas for Neue Galerie New York; 125 Candle Café;
126 (a) Bluestone Lane; 126 (b) Ben Hider; 127 Scott Ettin; 128 The Carlyle, A
Rosewood Hotel; 136 Levain Bakery; 137 Jonathan Bumble; 138 (a), 139 Bar
Boulud/M. Hom; 139 (b) Bar Boulud/E. Laignel; 138 (b), 139 (a, c) Peacefood;
140 Manhattan Cricket Club; 141 (a,b) ZUMA Press, Inc. / Alamy Stock Photo;
146 Andrew Morales/Life in Reverie; 150 (a), 151(a, c, e) Tastings Social present
Mountain Bird; 151 (b,d) One Hungry Jew; 152 (b, c) Sugar Hill Creamery; 153
Rob Zucker; iv-v (e), 158 (a) Catbird; 158 (b) Isabelle Raphael; 159 (a, c) Catbird;
159 (b) Isabelle Raphael; 162 George Padilla/Okonomi; 163 Mel Barlow; 164 (a),
165 (a,c,d,e, f) Maison Premiere; 170 (a) Pas Mal; 171 Anna Williams; 172 (a),
173 (b, c, e) Five Leaves; 172 (b), 173 (a, d, f) Bakeri; 174 Remy Amezcua; 175
Milk and Roses; 176-177 (a) Torst; 176-177 (b) Northern Territory; 182 b) Friends;
186 Roberta's; 185 Better Than Jam; 187 Eyal Yassky-Weiss; 188 (a) Michael
Tulipan; iv-v (a, k), 196-197 Home Studios; 198 Vicky Wasik; 199 Saraghina;
200 (a) Walter's; 200 (b), 201 (a,c,e) Cameron Holmes; 201 (b, d, f) Walter's
and Karasu; 206 Brooklyn Superhero Supply Company; 208 Marche rue Dix;
209 Paul Takeuchi; 210 Evan Sung; 211 Anne Massoni; 212-213 (a) Chavela's;
iv-v (g), 212-213 (b) Butter and Scotch, Kent Meister; 219 (a) Goose Barnacle;
220 (a) Colonie; 222-223 Ingalls Photography; 224, 225 (a) Henry Public; 225
(b) Floyd; 231 Jessica Antola; 232 Refinery; 234 (a), 235 (a, c) Miguel Herrera;
236 Buttermilk Channel; 237 June Wine Bar; 242 Russell Whitmore; iv-v (l), 243
Ray Spears; iv-v (b), 244-245 (a) The Good Fork; 246 (a), 247 (a, c) Ken Goodman;
248 (b) Seaborne; 261 Paul Wagtouicz.

ABOUT THE AUTHOR

Pip has lived in New York since 2011, having fallen hopelessly in love with the vibrant city during a visit in 1998. Even with a wonderful career at *The Sydney Morning Herald* and a home at Bondi Beach, the seduction of the Big Apple's cultural, political and intellectual life proved irresistible.

As a journalist there, she has profiled leaders in the arts, entertainment and design, worked for many years as a news editor and reporter, and as Managing Editor for legendary editor Tina Brown, whose Women in the World summits vigorously promote the empowerment of women and girls.

Pip currently lives in a five-storey Italianate brownstone in Brooklyn, whose convivial residents are all philosophers and writers (and cats). As lovely as that is, there's no place that warms her ardently Australian soul like summer weekends on a sand spit in the middle of the ocean, in the tiny community of Lonelyville, Fire Island.

ACKNOWLEDGEMENTS

A huge debt of gratitude to Hardie Grant's patient and talented editors and designers; in particular Melissa Kayser, Megan Cuthbert, Nick Tapp, Emily Maffei, designer Michelle Mackintosh, typesetter Megan Ellis and the impeccably thorough and always enthusiastic Alice Barker.

Boundless thanks to Lisabeth During, Ross Poole and all at Casa Pacifica, for your cheer, insight, and companionship throughout the duration of this project. Also to Betsy Wollheim and Peter, Lily and Zoe Stampfel; Wendy Laister and Finn Laister-Smith, and Lily Brett and David Rankin, for sharing your beautiful homes with me over the years.

Love always to my New York crew – Nikki Di Falco, Anton Monsted, Konstantine Pinteris, Isabelle Raphael, Tim Slade, Taylor and Franny Valentine, Phoebe Weekes and Edwina White – who I've explored the city with and who share this *amour fou*. Indelible memories were also made with Beatrice Claflin, Micaela Cronin, Liz Doran, Joshua Marston, Adam Rorris and Nairn Scott, and many of our special places are in this book. To everyone who came through and got in touch – you gave me fresh eyes on the city and treasured experiences.

This book is for Mia and Sasha, who I've imagined here hundreds of times, and for my nieces and nephews – Joseph, Jennifer, Charlotte, Isabella and William. Follow your dreams.

Published in 2018 by Hardie Grant Travel, a division of Hardie Grant Publishing

Hardie Grant Travel (Melbourne)
Building 1, 658 Church Street
Richmond, Victoria 3121

Hardie Grant Travel (Sydney)
Level 7, 45 Jones Street
Ultimo, NSW 2007

www.hardiegrant.com/au/travel

This maps in this publication incorporate data from: © OpenStreetMap contributors

OpenStreetMap is made available under the Open Database License: http://opendatacommons.org/licenses/odbl/1.0/. Any rights in individual contents of the database are licensed under the Database Contents License: http://opendatacommons.org/licenses/dbcl/1.0/

© NYC Open Data – Department of Information Technology & Telecommunications (DoITT)
© NYC Open Data – Department of City Planning

Public data sets made available on the NYC Open Data Portal are provided for informational purposes. The City does not warranty the completeness, accuracy, content, or fitness for any particular purpose or use of any public data set made available on the NYC Open Data Portal, nor are any such warranties to be implied or inferred with respect to the public data sets furnished therein.

The City is not liable for any deficiencies in the completeness, accuracy, content, or fitness for any particular purpose or use of any public data set, or application utilizing such data set, provided by any third party.

A catalogue record for this
book is available from the
National Library of Australia

New York Precincts
ISBN 9781741175479

10 9 8 7 6 5 4 3 2 1

Publisher
Melissa Kayser

Project editor
Megan Cuthbert

Editors
Alice Barker and Nick Tapp

Research and writing assistance
Bernie and Jess Watt

Proofreader
Susan Paterson

Cartographer
Emily Maffei

Design
Michelle Mackintosh

Typesetting
Megan Ellis

Index
Max McMaster

Prepress
Megan Ellis and Splitting Image Colour Studio

Printed and bound in China by LEO Paper Group

Disclaimer: While every care is taken to ensure the accuracy of the data within this product, the owners of the data (including the state, territory and Commonwealth governments of Australia) do not make any representations or warranties about its accuracy, reliability, completeness or suitability for any particular purpose and, to the extent permitted by law, the owners of the data disclaim all responsibility and all liability (including without limitation, liability in negligence) for all expenses, losses, damages (including indirect or consequential damages) and costs which might be incurred as a result of the data being inaccurate or incomplete in any way and for any reason.

Publisher's Disclaimers: The publisher cannot accept responsibility for any errors or omissions. The representation on the maps of any road or track is not necessarily evidence of public right of way. The publisher cannot be held responsible for any injury, loss or damage incurred during travel. It is vital to research any proposed trip thoroughly and seek the advice of relevant state and travel organisations before you leave.

Publisher's Note: Every effort has been made to ensure that the information in this book is accurate at the time of going to press. The publisher welcomes information and suggestions for correction or improvement.

**A free digital download of the text and maps from this book is available at: https://goo.gl/sHdr3W
Just make sure to have this book handy, so you can answer some questions as proof of purchase.**